Tampico
Pueblo Viejo
Tampico el Alto
Barra de Chavarria
Alta Mira
J. Blanquilla
J. de Lobos
Tantoyuca
Tamiahua
Barra de Tanguijo
Tuxpan
Barra de Cazones
Papantla
Barra de Nautla
Nautla
Misantla
Pt. Delgada
Jalapa
Pt. Nacional
Vera Cruz
Medellin
Alvarado
Tlacotalpam
Cosamaloapan
Pachuca
Mexico
Tlaxcala
Puebla
Cuernavaca
Morelos
Morelia
Toluca
Hidalgo
Queretaro
San Luis Potosi
Rio Verde
Salvatierra
Chilpancingo
Acapulco
Ayutla
San Marcos
Tlapa
Oaxaca
Etla
Zimatlan
Ocotlan
Tehuantepec
Cuicatlan
Teotitlan
Tecomavaca
Huajuapam
Choapam
Villa Alta
Zempoaltepec
Pt. Escondido
Pochutla
Sierra Madre
Mezcala
Iguala
Tlachapa
Pt. de Papanoa
Boca de Mitla
Boca del Nexpa
Llanos de Tomalhuacan
Tlascala
Los Angeles
Vera
Zapotecas
Chinantla
Oaxaca
Guaxaca
S. Ildefonso
Tabasco
Tabasco
V. Hermosa
Palenque
R. Guazacoalco
Chiapa
Ciudad real
Chiapa
Comitlan
Tecoantepec
Campeach
Tampico

R. de las Nacas

LEON

R. de las Palmas

R. Sauceda

SCAY

Palos

I. Salso

Tanxipa

PANUCO

Saludad

rango

Manille

Chichemecas

Rio Verde

Tanteo

or

Pamico

Sacotecas

Sacotecas

S. Iago

Tampico

S. Luis de Potosi

Taucaca

GUASTECA

Sichu

Vexla

Teutl

Palioque

Nilotepec

Barania

Felipe

S. Luis de la Paz

Meztitlan

R.

Leon S.Miguel

Queretaro

Tuspa

Pachuca

Tula

Otumba

Achiachico

L. Chapala

Salaya

Chotula

Segura Frontera

Istlan

Salamanca

MICHOACAN

Zapodan

Mecho acan

MEXICO

Tlascala

los Angeles

Colima

Pasquaro

Turiquato

Cuernaca

Tenaca

Ver

Melin

Guanato

Tasco

Atenango

Zaspe

Zacatula

Zumpango

MEXTLA

Chinantla

Acapulco

Nexpa

Sihula

Petatlan

R. de los Yopes

Isquitepec

Oax

GU

S. Pedro

MEXICO CITY
COCKTAILS

AN ELEGANT COLLECTION OF OVER 100 RECIPES INSPIRED BY THE CITY OF PALACES

MARTHA MÁRQUEZ

CIDER MILL PRESS

BOOK PUBLISHERS

MEXICO CITY COCKTAILS

ISBN-13: 978-1-40034-264-8
ISBN-10: 1-4003-4264-3

This book may be ordered by mail from the publisher. Please include $5.99 for postage and handling. Please support your local bookseller first!

Books published by Cider Mill Press Book Publishers are available at special discounts for bulk purchases in the United States by corporations, institutions, and other organizations. For more information, please contact the publisher.

Cider Mill Press Book Publishers
"Where good books are ready for press"
501 Nelson Place
Nashville, Tennessee 37214
cidermillpress.com

Typography: Block Berthold Condensed, Copperplate, Sackers, Warnock

Photography credits on page 305

Printed in India

24 25 26 27 28 REP 5 4 3 2 1

First Edition

CONTENTS

INTRODUCTION

Ruins of the Main Temple (Huēyi Teōcalli in the Náhuatl language)

History of Mexico City's Cocktail Culture

Imagine being an eyewitness to a pre-Hispanic ceremony and hearing music created from shells, whistles, drums, and rattles combined with the chanting of priests. The slow movements of the vibrant colors of exotic feathers in the plumes capture your eye with the mysticism of the scene. The smell is an unforgettable aroma of copal, cacao, maize, and an agave specially fermented to prepare *octli* or *pulque*, "the beverage of the gods."

For the Aztecs and Mayas, religion was the center of their lives; they were completely dedicated to their gods. They believed that offering tributes and expressing gratitude to them with special rituals would provide them with protection and blessings for their people. Thus, some fermented beverages were considered sacred and seen as an essential part of keeping balance between heaven and earth.

Even though the concept of a cocktail, as we understand it today, didn't exist back in Tenochtitlán, Chichén Itzá, or Palenque, there were a variety of fermented beverages created from native plants that were often mixed with herbs or flowers in order to create a more complex flavor. Some of these are still produced in Mexico with recipes that have been passed down from generation to generation. For example, *balché* is a mysterious Mayan beverage prepared from the bark of the balché tree mixed with honey and fermented for several days, after which extra ingredients can be added, like chile peppers or anise. It was believed that drinking balché produces magical powers and cures illnesses with its medicinal properties.

Nochoctli, or *colonche,* is a fermented beverage made from the cactus fruit known as *tuna,* which has a sweet and sour flavor and a slightly viscous texture. *Tejuino,* which means "heartbeat" in Náhuatl, is a bittersweet maize "beer" sweetened with *piloncillo (*a kind of unrefined cane sugar) and served chilled with lemon juice and salt.

Tepache is a refreshing fermented beverage made with pineapple, brown sugar, and spices; it has a fizzy characteristic and these days it's common for merchants to add a dash of rum to it. *Tesgüino* is a sour low-alcohol beverage made from fermented chewed maize; it has played an important spiritual role for the indigenous people of Mexico.

The most well-known pre-Hispanic fermented beverage is pulque, which, during the Aztec empire, was used as a form of currency for trading goods. The pulque is obtained from the heart of the Salmiana or Americana Agave by the *tlachiqueros,* which means "those who extract the eau-de-vie from the mother earth" in Náhuatl. Its importance in the heritage of Mexican beverage culture is undeniable; today, it's enjoying a rebirth thanks to food and drink enthusiasts who are willing to experiment and return to their roots.

Tenochtitlán and the Beginning of the Colonial Era

On August 13, 1521, Tenochtitlán fell after a siege when it was invaded by the Spanish conqueror Hernán Cortés and his allies: the Tlaxcaltecs (a powerful enemy of the Aztecs), Totonacs, Huexotzicans, and Texcocans. This episode marked the end of Mesoamerican history and the beginning of the colonial era.

Map engraved by Samuel Estradanus in 1618, from *Sitio, naturaleza y propiedades de la Ciudad de México,* by Diego Cisneros

During this period, wine and brandy were imported from Europe and they were mainly consumed by the colonial elites. Later on, vineyards and distilleries were established in the New World with promising results, until the Spanish crown prohibited the production of wine in Nueva España. Rumor has it this ban provoked one of the main drivers behind the independence movement led by the priest Miguel Hidalgo y Costilla, who lacked consecration wine.

While the pre-Hispanic drinks continued to be made by the locals, the arrival of the Spaniards brought regulations and taxation to the alcoholic beverages. However, the Spanish also brought with them distillation techniques learned from the Arabs, leading to the creation of a new spirit in this mestizo culture, the "wine of agave." Can you guess which spirit I am referring to?

Fruits of the Agave

No history of the cocktails in Mexico would be complete without a nod to Mexico's world-renowned spirits: tequila and mezcal. So, it's time for the Legend of Mayahuel, the Aztec goddess of agave and fertility.

As the story goes, a thunderstorm once struck and burned an agave plant. Afterward, a mystical sweet liquid with relaxing and euphoric effects emerged from within. It was believed that the agave plant was created from Mayahuel's body, and that this event was a message from the gods. This legend gave rise to the myth of the *mexcalli.*

The word *mexcalli* derives from the Náhuatl—*Metl* ("agave") and *Ixcalli* ("cooked")—and can be used to describe all of the alcoholic beverages produced from cooked agaves, known as mezcals. Mexico has more than 200 different kinds of agaves; tequila is just one kind of mezcal produced from the Blue Weber Agave, and the mezcals can be produced from more than fifteen other popular agave species. All tequilas are mezcals, but not all mezcals are tequilas.

The tequila we know today was shaped by the techniques the Spanish brought to Mexico. The first person to give it the name "tequila" instead of "wine of agave" was Don Cenobio Sauza, owner of Casa Sauza, one of the most important tequila producers. The name refers to the location in the state of Jalisco where tequila was first produced.

Mexico City, Early Taverns, and the Paloma

The cocktail scene in Mexico City has a rich and fascinating history that has its roots in the vibrant cantinas of the nineteenth century. It was there that the first mixes of aguardientes, tequilas, and mezcals were introduced. Nevertheless, the taverns and pulquerías were the first locations in which men would gather to socialize and have a drink before cantinas were established. (I refer to men because it was not socially acceptable for a Mexican woman to be seen in a cantina until approximately the mid-twentieth century.) These places were typically rustic and simple, and mainly established in the center of Mexico City.

By the mid-1800s, the social and drink scene had evolved and places such as El Nivel, La India, La Jalisciense, and La Peninsular began to gain popularity. But it was in 1876, when Bar La Opera opened its doors in the heart of Mexico City during the presidency of

Bar La Opera

Porfirio Díaz, that it took off. (Diaz is a significant figure in Mexican history, and he has been known for his admiration of French culture—he's actually buried in Montparnasse Cemetery in Paris.) This bar reflects the French influence on the Mexican bar scene at the time and it was a popular place among artists, politicians, and intellectuals. It's been a long-standing rumor that the Mexican Revolution was even planned over tequilas at La Opera, which the bartenders there may tell you about when you visit. Interesting, right?

During this period, one could escape to a sunny beach in Mexico with just one sip of the Paloma, or "dove" in English. This delightful cocktail was invented by Javier Delgado Corona at the bar La Capillita in Jalisco in 1860. It's a perfect balance of sweet and salty, but with a citrusy and strong taste. The salt rim provides the first flavor, and when complemented with a sparkling grapefruit juice soda, it takes you to paradise. Today, the Paloma has become a cult classic Mexican drink, and you can even find ready-to-drink versions in convenience stores across Mexico.

Twentieth-Century Mexico City and the Margarita

During the twentieth century, Mexico City was characterized by a blend of local traditions and international influences. A new wave of migrants arrived between the 1920s and 1940s, including not only Europeans, but also Americans, Arabs, and Asians. They brought new ingredients that were adapted into Mexican liquid gastronomy. This was the time when the cocktail culture began to flourish in the "City of Palaces" (a name referring to the grand architecture of Mexico City), and when the Margarita was created.

The Margarita is one of the most popular tequila-based cocktails in the world. We all love the perfect combination of tequila, triple sec,

Santo Domingo, 1933   **Hat market, 1927**

lemon juice, and salt. Its origin and authorship, however, remain unclear. Some claim it was named after Margarita Henkel, the daughter of the German ambassador in Mexico during the 1940s, while others say it was created by Carlos "Danny" Herrera as a special tailor-made cocktail for the actress Marjorie King, who was allergic to most of the ingredients used in cocktails, except for those used in the Margarita. Despite the origin, we can all agree that it's one of the most refreshing cocktails and a distinctive representative of Mexican drinks.

As Mexico City began to grow, so did its drinking culture. Hotel bars, such as the London-style Phone Bar in the legendary Hotel Geneve, began to attract more sophisticated customers with their elegant settings and high-quality, internationally known cocktails such as Martinis and Negronis. Soon bartenders in different locations were conjuring up their own creations for their clientele as a tailor-made service, experimenting with new ingredients and techniques that reflected their own history.

CDMX on the Global Cocktail Scene

Over time, Mexico City has become home to a thriving community of bartenders, mixologists, and cocktail bars, including rooftops and speakeasies that have redefined the cocktail scene. I love speakeasies in particular for their mysterious atmosphere, hidden entrances, and codes that transport you back to the Prohibition Era in the United States. If you share my love for theme bars, you cannot miss Hanky Panky, a speakeasy disguised behind a colorful Oaxacan *fonda*, which is a small traditional Mexican restaurant. If you are looking for the epicenter of this exciting industry, head to neighborhoods like La Roma, Juárez, Polanco, and La Condesa where you'll find endless aromas, flavors, textures, garnishes, and spirits to explore.

International recognition has also been important for the development of the cocktail culture in CDMX. In the 2023 list of the World's 50 Best Bars, four Mexican bars were recognized for their innovation, beverage design, cocktail menu, hospitality, and quality. Leading the list was Handshake Speakeasy at number 3, followed by Licorería Limantour at 7, Hanky Panky at 22, and Baltra Bar at 45. Other bars made the top 100: Rayo placed 72 and Kaito del Valle 81.

Furthermore, there has been a growing interest in the professionalization of the industry, with the establishment of bartender academies that offer a wide range of courses from basic techniques to advanced mixology. International and local spirits brands have also collaborated with Mexican bartenders, creating opportunities and space for contests, workshops, and tastings. Streaming platforms such

as Amazon have created shows like *The Ultimate Mixologist* and fairs like Barra Mexico have provided a way to educate, promote, and enrich the cocktail scene with new ideas.

All the history, evolution, and initiatives developed in Mexico City have contributed to its worldwide recognition, making it a must-visit destination for cocktail enthusiasts. So, get ready, pack your bags, and immerse yourself in a truly unique and unforgettable cocktail experience in Mexico City.

The Resurgence of Ancestral Spirits

Without a doubt, tequila and mezcal have played a significant role in shaping the city's cocktail history, reflecting the richness of Mexican gastronomy and cultural heritage in their use. However, ancestral Mexican spirits such as raicilla, sotol, bacanora, pox, and charanda have experienced a resurgence, gaining popularity among beverage designers, and are increasingly being used as main ingredients in the most important cocktail hotspots in the city. For more on the differences of these spirits, refer to the chart in the section titled "Setting Up and Stocking Your Own Mexico City Bar."

Pulque

The Rediscovery of Native Ingredients

Bartenders in CDMX are also exploring the use of native ingredients like corn, ancho chiles, and poblano chiles to create exciting new beverages that reflect the local terroir. This trend has led to the creation of delicious new liquors like Nixta Licor de Elote and Ancho Reyes, which add depth and complexity to cocktails. One such cocktail to try is the Gavilán Reyes, a refreshing drink made with ancho chile liquor, grapefruit juice soda, lemon, and salt. It's like a Paloma but with a lower alcohol by volume (ABV) and a spicy touch.

Unexpected liqueurs made from flowers and fruits also offer rich and aromatic notes to the mixology. For example, Huana is a Mexican liqueur produced from soursop (guanabana), while Damiana Liqueur adds an aphrodisiac element to drinks. Xtabentún is a delicate liqueur crafted from herbs, anise, and honey that symbolizes the essence of the region's cocktail heritage.

Mexico's spicy roots are present in innovative concoctions that celebrate the country's vibrant flavors, adding a distinctive and complex dimension to drinks. Whether you are in a Mexico City bar or having a homemade cocktail, you can find infused spirits with the fiery heat of chile peppers like chiles de árbol, jalapeños, or even habaneros (the spiciest), as well as glasses rimmed with Tajín (ground chile peppers, lime, and salt) to add a zesty component to a drink. Even chile pepper garnishes are on the rise. Worm salt, aka *sal de gusano*, is made from ground dried worms and is usually mixed with salt and chili powder. It is used to rim the glasses of some cocktails and served alongside orange slices to complement shots of mezcal. Finally, don't forget about the sweet and spicy notes of chamoy and Miguelito el Original, two spice mixes often used to create unique flavor combinations in cocktails.

Mexico is a kingdom of flavors, where cacao, corn, and chile peppers evoke memories of ancient Aztec and Mayan traditions, and the abundance of flowers, herbs, and tropical fruits showcase the rich diversity of flavors and culinary traditions found in Mexican mixology.

Sustainability

Sustainability has become a significant challenge for bar owners, who are becoming increasingly conscious of the ingredients they consume and their origins. To support local producers and reduce their carbon footprint, some bar owners and mixologists have begun incorporating locally sourced ingredients like hibiscus, tamarind, or native flowers as garnishes. By using fresh ingredients, bartenders not only improve the quality of the cocktail but also contribute to the local economy. Likewise, the practice of reusing fruits and vegetables has become popular, reducing production costs and minimizing waste. For example, cucumber peels, once considered waste, are now used to create cucumber syrups or garnishes, along with other ingredients such as lemons and pineapples.

Bespoke Cocktails

Another trend in CDMX is the rise of cocktails crafted for individual customers. These drinks tend to use a wide variety of local and imported ingredients that create delicious cocktails that are also visually stunning, with elaborate garnishes, smoke, and specially designed glassware made to resemble birds, octopi, or even skulls (get ready to take pictures of the most aesthetic Instagrammable drinks!).

What's Popular Now in CDMX

Mexico City's cocktail scene is in a continuous evolution. Spritzes—the Aperol Spritz, St-Germain Spritz, or ones made with local liqueurs—are popular for day-drinking on sunny terraces and rooftops. Gin & Tonics in which botanicals and tonic water can be customized to the customer's preference are also popular. Digestifs, often variations of the traditional Carajillo made from espresso and Licor 43, are gaining popularity. The Mezcalita is another trendy yet classic Mexican cocktail, which combines the smoked notes of mezcal with a variety of tropical fruits like watermelon, guava, lychee, and mandarin, as well as other citrus notes.

But perhaps the most prominent trend in Mexico City today is a shift toward minimalism. By minimalism, I mean a wiser and intentional use of ingredients, where clarifications and quality over quantity are emphasized in spirits, liquors, and even in ice with a focus on highlighting the natural flavors and textures of each ingredient. The focus on the beauty of the simple, the elegant, balanced, and refined not only honors the purity of Mexican ingredients but also moves toward a conscientious consumption and sustainable cocktails environment.

How to Drink Like a "Chilango"

Chilango is a colloquial term used to refer to people who were born in Mexico City, and if you are ready to enjoy the vibrant CDMX cocktail scene, here are some tips to help you:

START OUT EASY. Instead of beginning with strong cocktails, try a Michelada as a first sip. A Michelada is a refreshing mix of beer, lemon juice, and salt. There are some variations, for example the Michelada Clamato adds tomato juice with clam and hot sauce to the mix, while the Michelada Cubana includes Maggi seasoning sauce, Worcestershire sauce, and hot sauce.

KARLA MELJEM, MIRELL RIVIELLO & MARIA TAPIA: THE ART OF LAS MICHELADAS

Delightful, citrusy, refreshing, and, of course, spicy, the Michelada is probably the first cocktail every Mexican tries. This unique concoction blends lime juice, salt, the kick of chili, sometimes sauces, and, of course, your beer of choice, becoming ideal on sunny days, rainy afternoons, and every moment in between. Mexico loves beer. In 2023, Mexicans consumed 70 liters of beer per capita, according to the National Institute of Statistics and Geography (INEGI). It is also the world's largest beer exporter.

In Mexico City, the Michelada takes on countless forms, each one reflecting the essence of the restaurants, neighborhoods, or personal choices. From the classic Michelada with Clamato, a popular tomato juice beverage blended with spices and clam juice, passing through the Michelada Cubana, which is a mixture of beer, lime juice, hot sauces, Maggi sauce, Worcestershire sauce, and salt, to Micheladas with shrimp, and even unexpected additions like gummy bears—Gummychelas—and then the famous Licuachelas, Mexico City offers all the variations.

These last ones aren't scared of adding ingredients. Served in a blender's glass (yes, you read that right), the Licuachelas include some gummies, chamoy, fruits or fruit juices, and sometimes even spirits like vodka or rum, giving the name to Licualocas or "crazy blenders."

Such is the beauty of Mexico, a country where culinary creativity knows no bounds, making it an ideal destination for those seeking the unexpected.

Karla Meljem (aka @karlasommelier), has gained renown for her youthful content on wine and spirits in Mexico City. However, she's not merely an average creator; she has achieved the impressive feat of passing the WSET 3 with merits and is currently studying the DipWSET. For those in the industry, this accomplishment speaks to the countless hours of study, preparation, and dedication involved. Here

Karla shares her list of must-have ingredients. "My perfect Michelada is rimmed with chamoy and a crust of caramelized *ajonjolí*, 100% clamato juice, freshly squeezed lime juice, a dash of Maggi and Worcestershire sauce, and a lot of Tabasco!"

Maria Tapia (aka @bonsvibants.mx), is dedicated to speaking to her audience as a friend, sharing insights on rating wines, spirits, and ideal dinner spots. For her, a perfect complement to beer, beyond lemon juice, is mezcal, and if you haven't tried this yet, consider it your sign. "I prefer to pair an artisanal beer with a *caballito*—a shot—of mezcal," she says. "It's about combining them on your palate, like a deconstructed cocktail."

In Mexico City and some other states of the country, it's common that once you ask for a mezcal combo with a beer, they offer you orange wedges sprinkled with chili, worm salt, or even grasshopper salt, but Maria has a thrilling pairing: fresh slices of green tomato. "Its flavor is surprisingly enhancing, bringing out the notes of the beer and mezcal," she says.

Mirell Riviello

Karla Meljem

Don't rule out the classics. "Definitely, the best way to enjoy a Michelada is keeping it simple," says renowned wine and tea sommelier Mirell Riviello (aka @mell.sommelier), a radio host and contributor in digital and print media in the gourmet industry. "For me the combination of lime juice and rimmed salt is just what every Michelada needs. We as Mexicans have the tradition of putting lime juice on everything—on tacos, corn, soup—so pairing it with typical coastal dishes is a daily

Maria Tapia

pairing. In addition to being refreshing, it is rich in vitamin C."

In case you were wondering, dear reader, my ideal Michelada includes Pacifico or Tecate beer with tomato juice, lemon juice, salt, pepper, Maggi sauce, Worcestershire sauce, lots of Tabasco, and a dash of vodka. It's like a Bloody Mary–inspired beer cocktail, but without the heavy texture of a fully tomato-based cocktail.

An ideal pairing involves more chili!! If there are chips with Valentina, Miguelito chili powder, lime juice, spicy crudités, or fruits with chili, it is bound to be an excellent pairing. Because even sweets, breads, veggies, chocolates, or anything you can name tastes better with chili!

TRY THE ICONS. The Paloma and the Margarita are both excellent choices for an introduction to Mexican cocktails. If you are looking for something new, the Naked & Famous is a must-try cocktail. Created in 2011 by Joaquin Simo in New York City, this mezcal-based cocktail is made of equal parts mezcal, Aperol, Yellow Chartreuse, and lemon juice. It has an interesting and unique flavor that can make you understand the great versatility of mezcal in beverage design.

TAKE A CLASS ON MEXICAN SPIRITS. Explore and taste the differences of all the local spirits produced in Mexico. Learn more about the various types of agaves and the distillation processes used to make each kind of tequila or mezcal. You can find masterclasses through Airbnb experiences, bar and restaurant workshops, or even with sommeliers.

VISIT A CANTINA. No Mexico City cocktail experience is complete without a visit to the traditional cantinas. These spots are often crowded with "amigos" enjoying themselves to the sound of mariachis, Mexican music, and lots of laughter. Don't forget to say "Salud!" ("Cheers!") with a *caballito de tequila* (shot of tequila) and enjoy the delicious cantina food.

GO BARHOPPING IN THE WORLD'S BEST BARS. Be prepared to experience the fine drinking of CDMX and cross off Licorería Limantour, Handshake Speakeasy, Hanky Panky, Baltra Bar, Rayo, and Kaito del Valle from your bucket list. Reservations recommended.

EMBRACE THE LIQUID GASTRONOMY OF RESTAURANTS. Most restaurants serve signature cocktails that complement their cuisine. You'll be gladly surprised by the diverse creations they have to offer.

"TODO CON MEDIDA, NADA CON EXCESO." Everything with moderation, nothing with excess. A popular saying that emphasizes the importance of balance. Remember to keep yourself hydrated.

Setting Up and Stocking Your Own Mexico City Bar

Probably by now you are in love with agave culture and all the endless combinations it offers. In order to set up your own "Tenochtitlán"-inspired home bar, you'll need to have different categories in mind: spirits, liqueurs, beers, mixers, glassware, and mixology tools. Be aware: it's gonna be spicy!

Spirit	Produced from	Produced in
Tequila	Agave Blue Weber	Jalisco, Nayarit, Michoacán, Guanajuato, and Tamaulipas
Mezcal	Agaves such as: *Angustifolia* Haw, *Potatorum, Cupreata, Karwinskii, Salmiana, Marmorata, Convallis*, and others	Oaxaca, Guerrero, Durango, Zacatecas, San Luis Potosí, Michoacán, Tamaulipas, and Puebla
Raicilla	Agaves such as: *Maximiliana* Baker, *Valenciana, Angustifolia* Haw, *Rhodacantha*, and *Inaequidens* Koch	Jalisco and Nayarit
Sotol	*Dasylirion wheeleri*	Chihuahua, Durango, and Coahuila
Bacanora	*Agave angustifolia Pacifico*	Sonora
Pox	Corn and sugarcane	Chiapas
Charanda	Sugarcane	Michoacán

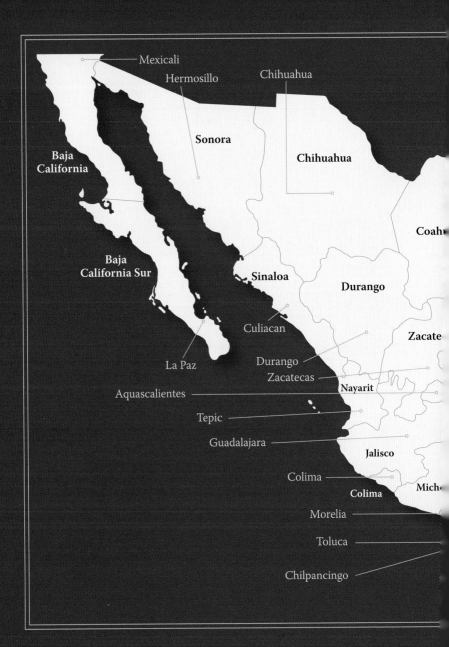

Mexicali

Hermosillo

Chihuahua

Sonora

**Baja
California**

Chihuahua

Coah

**Baja
California Sur**

Sinaloa

Durango

Culiacan

Zacate

Durango

La Paz

Zacatecas

Aquascalientes

Nayarit

Tepic

Guadalajara

Jalisco

Colima

Mich

Colima

Morelia

Toluca

Chilpancingo

Saltillo

Monterrey

Cuidad Victoria

San Luis Potosi

Merida

Tamaulipas

Guanajuato

Campeche

Luis
tosi

Queretaro

Pachuca

Yucatan

Mexico City

vo
n

Tlaxcala

**Quintana
Roo**

Hidalgo

Xalapa

Villahermosa

Tabasco

Campeche

Puebla

Veracruz

Chetumal

ero

Oaxaca

Chiapas

Cuernavaca Puebla

Oaxaca

Tuxtla Gutierrez

R de las Nacas

R LEON

R de las Palmas

R Sauceda

SCAY

rango

Palos

L. Salso

Tanxipa

PANUCO

Salua

Thunille

Chich emecas

Rio Verde

Tanteo

Sacotecas

Sacotecas

or S. Iago

Pamico

Sacotecas

S. Luis de Potosi

Taucaca

Tampico

GUASTECA

Teutl

rania

Sicru

Vexpa

Nilotepec

C

Felipe

S. Luis de la Paz

Palioque

Meztitlan

R.

Leon

St Miguel

Queretaro

Tusna

Tula

Pachuca

a Iaxara

Salaya

Counba

Achiaduca

L. Chapala

MECHO

Salamanca

Istlan

Chotula

Segura Frontera

Zapodan

Mecho acan

MEXICO

Tlascala

lina

Pasquaro

Cuernaxaca

los Angeles

Tenaca

Melin

Guanalo

Vera

Tasco

Atenango

S. zapo

MEXICO

Zumpango

CHIN

Chinantla

Zacatula

TLA

Petatlan

Nexpa

Oaxac

M
E

Sihula

R de los Yopas

Isquilepec

GUA

Acapulco

H

SHOPPING LIST

TEQUILA: Casa Dragones, Don Julio, 1900, DOBEL, Volcán
MEZCAL: Creyente, 400 Conejos, Ojo de Tigre, Amarás, Montelobos
BACANORA: Aguamiel, Sunora
SOTOL: Flor del Desierto, Hacienda de Chihuahua
RAICILLA: Las Ruinas
GIN: Las Californias, Diega, Condesa, Armónico, Ginstone
WHISKEY: Abasolo, Milpa
BEER: Corona, Tecate, Pacífico, Tempus, Carta Blanca, Noche Buena

MEXICAN LIQUEURS
Ancho Reyes Original Chile Liqueur
Ancho Reyes Verde Chile Liqueur
Nixta Licor de Elote
Damiana Liqueur
Casa D'Aristi Xtabentún Honey & Anise Liqueur
Kahlúa
Corajito Café con Licor Clásico

MIXERS
Squirt (caffeine-free grapefruit soda)
Tonic water
Soda water
Jarritos (soda, tamarind flavor)
Coconut water
Clamato (tomato cocktail)

MIXOLOGY TOOLS AND GLASSWARE
Shaker
Jigger
Barspoon
Kitchen scale
Muddler
Peeler
Paring knife
Mixing glass
Ice cube trays and large ice cube molds
Rocks glasses
Martini glasses

Oropel, in Roma Norte (see page 263)

JAZMÍN MARTÍNEZ, *FOOD POLICE*: DISCOVERING THE MEXICAN CANTINA

Inspired in the popular American show *Fashion Police*, Jazmín Martínez in 2015 created *Food Police* as a space for writing about the places she dined with the goal of telling the truth about what happens between plates. Over the years, Jazmín has become one of the few to turn a spotlight on the phenomenon of Mexican cantinas.

Traditionally, cantinas were mostly thought of as places of perdition and seediness. Now, however, there are many different types of cantinas: elegant ones, shabby ones, ones with snacks, ones without snacks, expensive ones, cheap ones . . . But they all have one thing in common: inside Mexican cantinas, social and economic status vanishes. You can find a high-ranking politician happily drinking and dining with someone who lives paycheck to paycheck and lives at a much lower social strata.

A curiosity to explore the unique atmosphere of real cantinas drove Jazmín. Her first cantina experience was at the historic La Opera in downtown Mexico City.

How would you define a cantina?

Cantinas are primarily spaces for drinking where social classes blur. You can also eat well-prepared Mexican food, listen to nostalgic music, play dominoes, or dance, but the real essence lies elsewhere. Some say that if there is no complimentary snack, it's not a cantina. Others, more close-minded, go so far as to say that if there are women, it's not a cantina. Back in

the day, women weren't allowed. I would say that the concept goes much further. The most important element of a cantina is the host. Without a host who is there, keeping an eye on the business, the customers, the kitchen, getting to know the regulars, understanding what and how they like their drinks, there is no cantina. A cantina must be a space that feels personal, where even if it's your first time, they make you feel like you've been there your whole life . . . I really like cantinas where you find someone willing to tell you the history of the place.

What is the importance of preserving the tradition of cantinas?

The story of Mexico was written over tequilas in cantinas, not in the offices of bureaucrats. During the Porfiriato (the era of Porfirio Díaz's presidency of Mexico, in the late nineteenth and early twentieth centuries) they were salons for the gentlemen of the regime; in the 1940s, a meeting point for intellectuals. The cantina is more than just a place for drinking; it's history, it's gastronomy—where else will you find so many ways to make a pork knuckle?

Cantinas are witnesses to another era, and they are our architectural heritage. It saddens me to know that with the current economic dynamics, it's becoming increasingly difficult for lifelong cantiñeros to continue, for example, giving away food with the purchase of a drink. The extortion by organized crime is another cancer that is ending them. Lack of knowledge too: young people sometimes don't know that cantinas exist, so they don't go. If we lose the cantina, we will lose the social dynamics of democracy that exist in them.

What are your favorite drinks and dishes when visiting a cantina?

A Cuba—a classic cocktail made with rum and Coke, with Bacardí Blanca Superior White Rum "pintadita" with a splash of Coke—and a torta. They make really good tortas in the cantinas.

Do you have any amusing or unexpected anecdotes from reviewing a cantina?

In Mexico, women couldn't enter cantinas until an official decree was issued in 1981. And in all my videos, there's never a shortage of irritated men eager for things to go back to how they were in the old days, before. It amuses me how much the male audience can get offended . . . Greetings to all of them.

What are five cantinas that everyone must visit, and what should they try there?

1. El Paraíso in Santa María la Ribera. Order the octopus torta in its ink.
2. Tío Pepe in Barrio Chino. There's no food, but their Bloody Marys are fantastic.
3. El Mirador in San Miguel Chapultepec. Try bartolo, one of the house desserts. It comes from an old bakery called La Vasca. Order it upon arrival because it runs out.
4. El Covadonga in Roma. The garlic soup is a beauty.
5. La Potosina. A lively cantina in the heart of the historic center of CDMX. It's run by a couple, and the lady has a talent for cooking homemade Mexican dishes. Go early, during the day, because this part of the center is not as touristy or friendly.

For more from Jazmín, check out @foodpolicemx or www.foodpolice.mx.

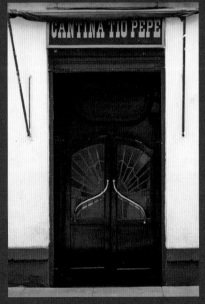

LAURA SANTANDER:
MEXICAN SPIRITS, COCKTAILS, AND GASTRONOMY

Unquestionably, Laura Santander is the best sherpa to guide you in the fascinating world of pairing. Her expertise and passion for the world of wine and spirits led her to become not only a certified sommelier by the Court of Master Sommeliers and a judge in competitions such as the México Selection by the Concours Mondial de Bruxelles, but also a master tequila maker, with vast experience in the restaurant and wine industries.

The key to a successful pairing is achieving balance, ensuring that neither the cocktail nor the spirit overshadows the food. Mexican spirits often have a high level of alcohol, and Mexican gastronomy can be complex and spicy, so it's important to consider a third element such as a chaser or an infusion to create a bridge between the spirit and the dish. "Not everything has to be strictly purist," Laura says. "Introducing complementary elements can aid in achieving harmonious pairings. For example, pairing a citrus profile tequila blanco with ceviche can be enhanced by a lemon infusion."

The most crucial thing to understand about Mexican spirits is that tequila is mezcal. "Beyond that, our vast country provides opportunities for different soil compositions, altitudes, and climates, leading to a variety of agaves. The geographical diversity in Mexico results in distinct characteristics; for instance, a region with higher altitude and cooler temperatures may yield agaves with citrusy and green aromas. There's a clear difference between them, much like wines."

That's the reason why, in Mexico, there are also Denominations of Origin (D.O.). A mezcal from Guerrero will have different characteristics than one from Oaxaca. Mexico's rich biodiversity, changing across specific regions, contributes to unique craft products.

It's possible to explore a wide range of spirits beyond just tequila, such as raicilla, sotol, bacanora, and pox—each is unique. "It's essential to understand the significant cultural influence on each spirit's production, not only in terms of empirical processes but also the cultural heritage embedded in Mexican distillation," says Laura. "This traditional and artisanal approach sets us apart, and it's crucial to pass on this knowledge."

When it comes to creating your own cocktails from Mexican spirits, Laura advises starting "with elements you are familiar with, things that are close to you, things you know exactly how they taste." Then go from there. "Does it need a bitter touch, more acidity? What acids do I know? I have this fruit that is a bit more acidic, add a bit of it—trial and error. Lastly, consider the ice dilution level and get ready to take a deep dive into Mexican traditions and spirits."

What are the four things everyone should know when getting into Mexican spirits?

1. Don't limit yourself to just one spirit. Avoid getting fixated on trends; explore different categories and types.
2. Be open to trying spirits from different states. Diversify your palate by exploring beyond familiar options.
3. Prioritize your health. Not all roadside mezcal or spirits sellers offer safe and quality products. Stick to certified ones.
4. If you think you know a lot about Mexican spirits, think again. The world of Mexican spirits is vast and diverse, requiring continuous learning.

A common misconception is that pairings are only about contrast, but understanding the predominant flavor in the dish is key. Consider the intensity of flavors and choose a cocktail with a medium intensity level. Focus on citrusy elements like mandarin, orange, or lime and address the texture of the dish. For greasy dishes, incorporate astringent elements in the cocktail. Experiment with complementary flavors and textures, maintaining a balance to enhance the overall dining experience.

How do you think the smoky notes of mezcal can complement the elements of a dish?

Many of our sauces and moles come from ingredients that have been roasted or toasted. It's a successful pairing because you can immediately match the toasted to the smoky, from chocolate to spicy.

CENTRO HISTÓRICO

CACTUS

OPERA

VOLCANITA

CANTARITO

TETÉ

TU VOZ

KALUZ 3.0

CATEDRAL

The essence of Mexico is in its streets, its markets, its cantinas, its flavors, its corns, its chiles, its pulque, and its mezcals. A country full of color and surprises. "Mexico is an endless field of steel blue–tinted maguey plants and crowns of yellow thorns," as Chilean poet Pablo Neruda wrote in his 1974 poem "I confess I have lived."

It began in downtown CDMX or "Centro," in ancient Tenochtitlán, "with its nopal, eagle, and serpent," its rituals and spiritual concoctions. Then came the historic cantinas such as La Opera and much-awarded restaurants such as Balcón del Zócalo, followed by the scene of today. Here, you can still taste and touch history through all its colonial architecture, beverages, cocktails, gastronomy, and landmarks. Welcome to the City of Palaces!

CACTUS

BALCÓN DEL ZÓCALO
AV. 5 DE MAYO #61 COL. CENTRO,
ALCALDÍA CUAUHTÉMOC

Cactus was meticulously crafted to challenge the preconceptions often associated with pulque, a traditional Mexican alcoholic beverage crafted from fermented agave sap. Pulque's distinctive taste deters some people from trying it. However, Héctor Mariche Morales ingeniously discovered an innovative approach to reintroduce this unique beverage by exploring various techniques and textures in the nopal cactus. The result is a spring cocktail that accentuates the importance of acidity prevalent in this traditional drink.

GLASSWARE: Black clay cup

GARNISH: Dehydrated nopal cactus

- 3 oz. | 90 ml Curado de Nopal (see recipe)
- 1 oz. | 30 ml mezcal espadín
- 1 oz. | 30 ml Kefir (see recipe)
- ½ oz. | 15 ml bianco vermouth
- Barspoon Hydrated Chia (see recipe)

1. Combine all of the ingredients in a cocktail shaker filled with ice.

2. Shake vigorously until chilled.

3. Strain the cocktail into a black clay cup filled with ice.

4. Garnish with dehydrated nopal cactus.

CURADO DE NOPAL: Blend pulque with Dehydrated Nopal (see recipe) and agave nectar.

KEFIR: Feed bulgur wheat grains with whole milk and let them ferment for 48 hours to achieve the correct fermentation.

HYDRATED CHIA: In a container, add 100 grams (about ½ cup) chia to 1 liter (4 cups) natural water and let it rest for at least 3 hours.

DEHYDRATED NOPAL: Set the dehydrator to 140°F (60°C). Slice nopal into strips approximately 2 inches long and line them on a dehydrator tray. Load the tray into the dehydrator and leave it for 24 hours.

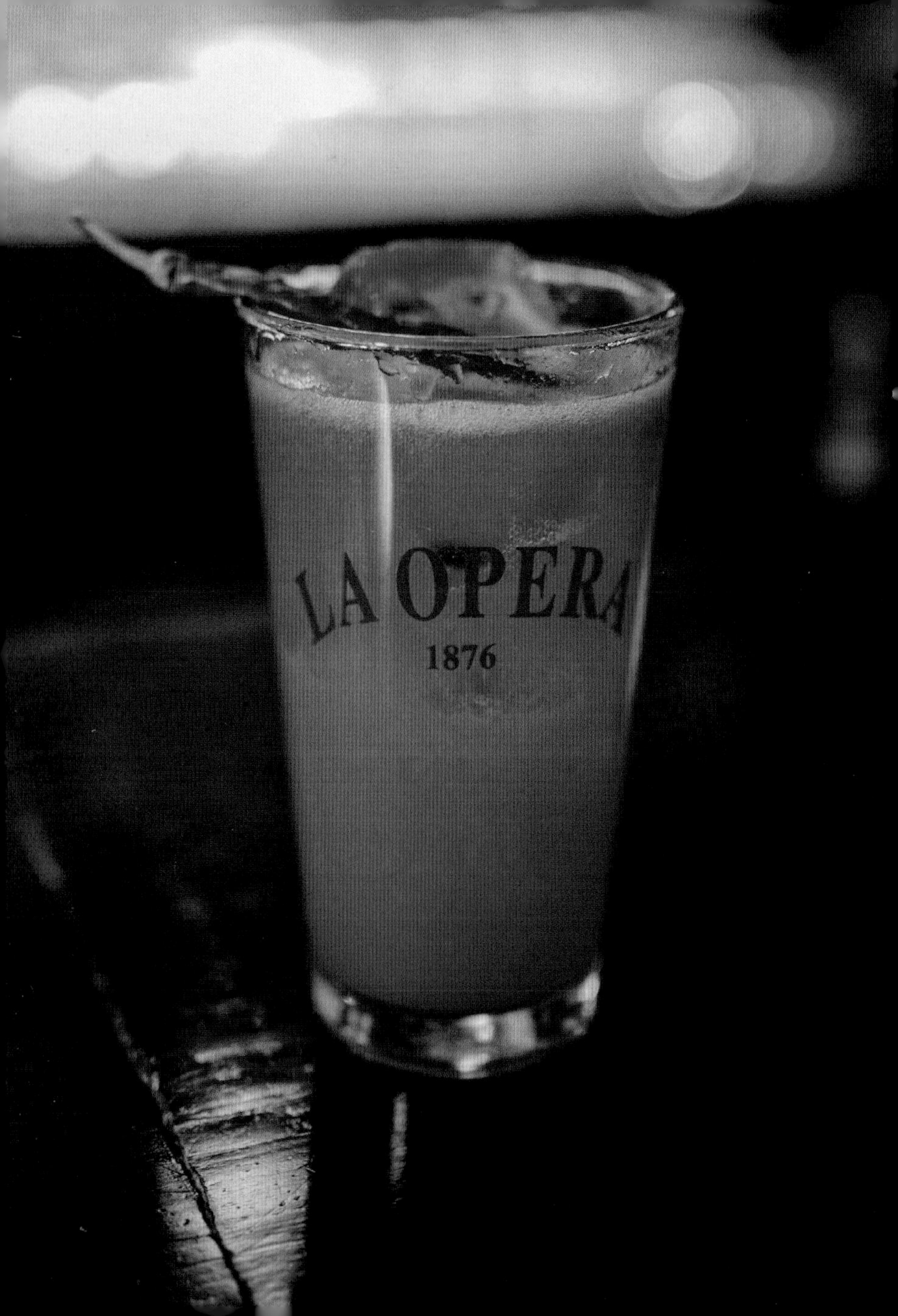
LA OPERA
1876

OPERA

One of Mexico's most iconic bars, established in 1876, Bar La Opera has been witness to numerous historic moments, drawing together political, cultural, and artistic circles of Mexico City. The bar boasts an impressive size and intricately carved woodwork, dating back to 1900 when it was brought from New Orleans. Next time you visit it, look up at the ceiling—you'll see a bullet hole left by Pancho Villa.

GLASSWARE: Pilsner glass

GARNISH: Dried chile de árbol

- 2 oz. | 60 ml Strawberry Concentrate (see recipe)
- 1 oz. | 30 ml tequila
- 1 oz. | 30 ml fresh lime juice
- 1 oz. | 30 ml simple syrup
- 1 oz. | 30 ml light beer, to top
- Tabasco sauce, to taste

1. Combine all of the ingredients, except for the light beer and Tabasco sauce, in a cocktail shaker filled with ice.

2. Shake vigorously until chilled.

3. Pour the contents of the shaker into a pilsner glass filled with ice.

4. Top with light beer and add Tabasco drops.

5. Garnish with dried chile de árbol.

STRAWBERRY CONCENTRATE: Blend fresh strawberries until smooth, and then refine the texture by straining it through a fine sieve before using.

ISRAEL LARA, *BARES Y COCTELES*

Imagine being the public relations and communications director at the Four Seasons in Mexico City, overseeing Fifty Mils, a bar that in its first year was included in the extended list of the World's 50 Best Bars. By its second year, it topped the list—that's when Israel Lara noticed the absence of media focus on bars, cocktails, and liqueurs. Then it was during the pandemic that the need to stay connected through digital media became so important. Thus he created his platform *Bares y Cocteles*, which consists primarily of a podcast and a TikTok account.

The podcast focuses on the happenings in Mexico's and Latin America's bars, and features guest interviews. The TikTock account, @baresycocteles, targets consumers and cocktail enthusiasts who are wanting to learn how to prepare cocktails at home using the ingredients and tools they have available. His online presence has expanded onto YouTube and Instagram.

"Although rooted in the bars of the 1980s and traditions like Sunday Micheladas," Israel says, Mexico City's cocktail scene "has evolved significantly."

When do you think Mexico City arrived on the cocktail scene and why?

The boom of mixology in Mexico City was a gradual process marked by key events and the emergence of iconic bars like Limantour, Fifty Mils, and Hanky Panky, among others. These places not only gained international recognition, but also became training centers for talented bartenders. The support of the alcohol industry and events like World Class and Bacardí Legacy Global, as well as local events like Barra México, played a crucial role in this development. It was like a Big Bang, where everything was both cause and effect simultaneously.

What do you consider to be the most influential or iconic cocktail in CDMX in recent years?

The Margarita is an iconic drink of the city, universally enjoyed by connoisseurs and those new to mixology. It tastes like Mexico, and there are various interesting twists or variations. Limantour's Margarita al Pastor embodies both a very Mexican drink and the *tacos al pastor*, something characteristic of Mexico City. Globally, it links the Margarita with Mexico, and the Margarita al Pastor has become famous worldwide. Other notable mentions include the Negroni, with excellent versions in Mexico City, especially with mezcal, and the Dry Martini, an obsession for bartenders seeking perfection. Last but not least, the Cuba Libre, the drink of Mexicans for a long time.

What are the five cocktails that anyone visiting Mexico City should try?

The Margarita al Pastor at Limantour, the Negroni at Hanky Panky, the Dry Martini at Baltra, the Salt and Pepper at Handshake, and the Wilson at Casa Prunes.

What are your favorite ingredients or spirits in cocktails? What is your drink of choice?

It depends on the mood and occasion, but a cocktail with citrus, botanical notes, and a bitter touch suits me well. I enjoy cocktails that include Italian spirits like Campari, Cynar, or Amaro. I'll mostly order a Negroni or a Gin & Tonic.

There's no question that Mexican mixology has played a significant role in promoting the country's culture, flavors, and heritage, attracting and motivating visitors to come to this vibrant metropolis. For Israel, this can also be a challenge. "There is so much expectation when coming to Mexico that the biggest challenge is to exceed that level, and there is less room for error each time." At the same time, "Mexico is trendy not only for foreigners but also for Mexicans, creating opportunities to develop mixology in more places across the country. There are more proposals for bars in the interior of the republic, very well set up, but there is room for more as the demand and public interest continue to grow."

VOLCANITA

GRANA SABORES DE ORIGEN
SAN JERÓNIMO 35 COL. CENTRO,
ALCALDÍA CUAUHTÉMOC

Grana Sabores de Origen is a hidden culinary gem in Mexico City's downtown where the authentic Mexican flavors come alive in every bite—or sip. The Volcanita is the perfect cocktail for avocado lovers and to ease into an evening that includes fine drinking.

GLASSWARE: Martini glass

- **Chili powder, for the rim**
- **8 oz. | 240 ml Agua de Aguacate (see recipe)**
- **1 oz. | 30 ml Tequila Volcán Blanco**
- **Peppermint leaves, to taste**

1. Wet the rim of martini glass and dip it into chili powder.

2. Combine all of the ingredients in a blender and blend.

3. Pour the cocktail into the glass.

AGUA DE AGUACATE: Add one piece of Hass avocado, 4 limes, brown sugar, to taste, and 1 liter water to a blender. Blend to combine and reserve it.

CANTARITO

JARDÍN JUÁREZ
AV. CHAPULTEPEC 61 COL. CENTRO
ALCALDÍA CUAUHTÉMOC

The iconic Cantarito reflects the essence of the fairs popular throughout various Mexican states, where music, laughs, and fiesta vibes come together in celebration. This blend of citrus juices, chili powder, and tequila—crafted by Yazmín Estrada—makes it perfect for a sunny day with friends.

GLASSWARE: Clay cantarito mug

GARNISH: Grapefruit wedge, sprig of fresh rosemary

- Tajín, for the rim
- 2 oz. | 60 ml grapefruit juice
- 1½ oz. | 45 ml orange juice
- 1 oz. | 30 ml fresh lime juice
- 1½ oz. | 45 ml Mayorazgo Cristalino Tequila
- 2 oz. | 60 ml grapefruit soda, to top

1. Wet the rim of the clay cantarito mug with grapefruit and dip it in the Tajín.
2. Build the cocktail in the mug with an ice cube in the order listed, leaving out the grapefruit soda.
3. Top with grapefruit soda and stir to combine.
4. Garnish with a grapefruit wedge and a sprig of fresh rosemary.

TETÉ

NARDO COCKTAIL CLUB
VENUSTIANO CARRANZA 69, COL. CENTRO HISTÓRICO

Teté is the nickname for Teresa, and there's no Teresa more well known in Mexico's City downtown than the Cine Teresa. A peculiar cinema that first opened its doors in 1924 as a venue for silent black-and-white projections, it suddenly shifted its focus after acquiring a collection of XXX films. Rodolfo Domínguez, the cocktail creator, was inspired by the Porn Star Martini to craft this unique drink. Nardo's cocktails are unique: each one represents a different neighborhood from the downtown area, expressing their own essence in a complete liquid experience designed by Ramon Tovar.

GLASSWARE: Highball glass inside a popcorn box
GARNISH: Popcorn

- 1½ oz. | 45 ml Mexican gin
- 1 oz. | 30 ml Passion Fruit Pulp (see recipe on page 141)
- 1 oz. | 30 ml Lemon & Spearmint Oil (see recipe)
- ½ oz. | 15 ml fresh lime juice
- Cider, to top

1. Combine all of the ingredients, except the cider, in a mini tin filled with ice.
2. Shake vigorously until chilled and strain the cocktail into a highball and place it inside a popcorn box.
3. Top the cocktail with cider and close the highball.
4. Garnish with popcorn.

LEMON & SPEARMINT OIL: Add the zest of 15 lemons, 200 grams spearmint leaves, and 500 grams (1 pound) sugar into a 20 oz. capacity jar. Let it rest for 24 hours at room temperature. Add 300 ml (10 oz.) hot water to the mixture and let it rest for 30 minutes; strain through a fine sieve. Store it and reserve it.

FERNANDO ACEVEDO

In one of the world's largest cities, where every sip tells a story and each cocktail is a celebration of Mexican culture, Fernando Acevedo stands out. A mixologist with over fourteen years of experience, he won the Ruta Torres 15 with his signature cocktail, the Golden Egg.

Mexico City's cocktail scene has three advantages, Fernando says. "Mexicans are among the most service-oriented and charismatic people worldwide, which is essential for excellent service and hospitality," he says. "Secondly, we are rich in fruits, making our ingredients natural and affordable. Last but not least, our culture and traditions are authentic, serving as tools to infuse our cocktails with stories and myths, taking our mixology to the next level."

What do you think is the most representative ingredient or spirit of Mexico City? What do you believe is the flagship cocktail of CDMX?

The most representative spirit of CDMX at the moment is mezcal. If I had to choose a cocktail, I think it would be the Carajillo, although I'm not a fan. I prefer a mezcal Espresso Martini.

Have you noticed any emerging trends in mixology in Mexico City?

Clarified cocktails have stood out a lot.

How do you see the future of mixology in Mexico City? Is there a particular direction you think it's heading in?

I see it heading toward beverages with lower alcohol content.

What is your must-visit place to have a fine drinking experience in CDMX?

Nowadays, Handshake Speakeasy for me is one of the bars that has taken mixology to the next level. It's a place that leverages its ingredients, respects its customers, and pays attention to the smallest details in customer service.

TU VOZ

MALEFICIO SPEAKEASY
EZEQUIEL MONTES 73 COL. TABACALERA,
ALCALDÍA CUAUHTÉMOC

Maleficio is a speakeasy inspired by a cabaret theater where villains gather to enjoy a cocktail. Served in a mystical cauldron, this bewitching cocktail brings back memories of villains under the sea who, with an enchanted potion, will take your voice, or *tu voz*, in Spanish.

GLASSWARE: Crystal cauldron

GARNISH: Edible Black Coral (see recipe), Tea Pearls (see recipe)

- 2 oz. | 60 ml RumChata
- ½ oz. | 15 ml Chambord
- ½ oz. | 15 ml milk
- Dash lime juice

- ½ oz. | 15 ml Blackberry Syrup (see recipe)
- Drop edible violet food coloring

1. Combine all of the ingredients in a cocktail shaker filled with ice.

2. Shake vigorously until chilled.

3. Strain the cocktail into a crystal cauldron filled with sphere ice.

4. Garnish with Edible Black Coral and Tea Pearls.

BLACKBERRY SYRUP: Muddle 150 grams (about ¾ cup) blackberries and 150 grams (about ¾ cup) raspberries with 300 grams (10¾ oz.) sugar. Refrigerate the mixture for 24 hours, then add 150 ml (⅔ cup) hot water. Mix the syrup, strain it, and reserve it.

TEA PEARLS: Infuse 10 grams (2 tablespoons) Aruba herbal tea (pineapple, beetroot, papaya, strawberry, and vanilla) into 500 ml (2 cups) water for 5 minutes. Strain it and let it cool. Using a mixer, blend the infusion with 7 grams (2¼ teaspoons) sodium alginate until it becomes a slightly thick liquid and place the mixture in a plastic dropper. Add 7 grams (2¼ teaspoons) calcium chloride to 500 ml (2 cups) water, stir and refrigerate for 5 hours. Afterwards, drop the herbal tea and alginate solution into the water with calcium chloride to form the spheres. Remove the spheres from the water using a perforated spoon and rinse in clean water. Store them in herbal tea infusion or sugar water in the refrigerator.

EDIBLE BLACK CORAL: Using a mixer, blend 10 grams (1¼ tablespoons) flour, 60 ml (2 oz.) vegetable oil, 55 ml (almost 2 oz.) water, and 3 drops black edible food coloring. Strain the mixture. Place 20 ml (4 teaspoons) of the mixture into a hot pan over medium heat and cook it until water evaporates, forming a coral shaped tile.

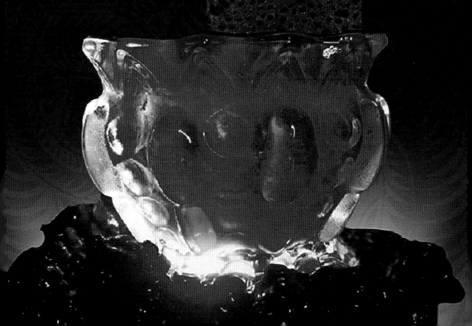

KALUZ 3.0

CAFÉ DE MUSEO KALUZ
HIDALGO 85 COL. CENTRO HISTÓRICO,
ALCALDÍA CUAUHTÉMOC

Crafted by mixologist Judith Rivera, this cocktail is a tribute to what this emblematic place represents. The symbiosis of European and Mexican cultures is reflected not only in the structure of the cocktail but also in the richness of its fragrance and flavor, which is complemented by the preserved facade of the former Augustinian convent of the Kaluz Museum.

* * *

GLASSWARE: Rocks glass

* Black salt, for the rim
* 1 oz. | 30 ml tequila
* 1 oz. | 30 ml pineapple juice
* 1 oz. | 30 ml fresh lime juice
* ½ oz. | 15 ml Campari
* ½ oz. | 15 ml Maleza Axiote Licor
* ½ oz. | 15 ml Passion Fruit Syrup (see recipe on page 142)

1. Wet the rim of a rocks glass and dip it into black salt.
2. Combine all of the ingredients in a cocktail shaker filled with ice.
3. Shake vigorously until chilled.
4. Strain the cocktail into the rocks glass.

CATEDRAL

TERRAZA CATEDRAL
REPÚBLICA DE GUATEMALA 4 COL. CENTRO,
ALCALDÍA CUAUHTÉMOC

Looking for the ideal cocktail that pairs with friends, sunglasses, and a terrace with a view on a sunny day? Your quest ends with this refreshing tropical drink created by Omar Torres. It's the signature drink of Terraza Catedral and undoubtedly the venue's most popular.

GLASSWARE: Syrah glass

GARNISH: Orange slices, fresh mint leaves, pink peppercorns

- 2 oz. | 60 ml gin
- 2 oz. | 60 ml Sweetened Passion Fruit Pulp (see recipe)
- 1 oz. | 30 ml simple syrup
- 1 oz. | 30 ml fresh orange juice

1. Combine all of the ingredients in a cocktail shaker with ice.

2. Shake vigorously until chilled.

3. Double-strain the cocktail over ice into a syrah glass.

4. Garnish with orange slices, fresh mint leaves, and pink peppercorns.

SWEETENED PASSION FRUIT PULP: Blend the pulp of 1 passion fruit pulp with 200 grams (7 oz.) sugar.

LA CONDESA

PIÑATA

MALAS DECISIONES

ROSSO JAMAICA

DOS PARADAS

MARÍA MEZCAL

DELETED SOULS

ROSA SPRITZ

NAMI SPRITZ

NUT FASHIONED

If there's a neighborhood that comes to mind for both chilangos and foreigners when looking for a place to eat and drink well in Mexico City, La Condesa is at the very top. Known for its greenery, Art Deco architecture, and a bohemian yet international atmosphere, it is a neighborhood where everybody loves to have a nice walk along charming streets after enjoying a delicious meal or simply enjoying a cocktail, mezcal, or glass of wine.

If you are curious about why it's called "La Condesa," let me tell you that it's named after the Countess of Miravalle, or La Condesa de Miravalle, María Magdalena Dávalos de Bracamontes y Orozco de Trebuesto, a rich widow of the eighteenth century. The countess owned more than seventy haciendas in Michoacán as well as where Roma and Condesa neighborhoods are established today. There are also rumors that she had a lover who was a friar who later poisoned her. Probably a myth!

Well, there you go: an interesting icebreaker fact to share next time you visit La Condesa.

PIÑATA

BIJOU DRINKERY ROOM
AV. SONORA 189 -B, COL. HIPÓDROMO CONDESA,
ALCALDÍA CUAUHTÉMOC

It all starts with a Rubik's cube menu, which you can twist to create more than 80,000 cocktail combinations. One of them is the iconic Mexican Piñata, symbolizing the seven deadly sins, its color representing temptation.

GLASSWARE: Nick & Nora glass

GARNISH: Dehydrated pineapple slice, Cilantro Air (see recipe)

- 1 oz. | 30 ml mezcal espadín
- 1 oz. | 30 ml Pineapple Cheong (see recipe)
- ¾ oz. | 22.5 ml oloroso sherry
- ¼ oz. | 7.5 ml Pineapple Lactofermento (see recipe)

1. Chill a Nick & Nora glass. Add all the ingredients to a mixing glass filled with ice.

2. Stir until chilled.

3. Strain the cocktail into the chilled Nick & Nora.

4. Garnish with a dehydrated pineapple slice and Cilantro Air.

PINAPPLE CHEONG: Peel a pineapple and cut it into pieces. Vacuum-seal the pieces with 500 grams (1 pound) sugar and 2 grams (¼ teaspoon) salt, then sous vide the mixture for 2 hours at 131°F (55°C). Strain the mixture, bottle it, and refrigerate it.

PINEAPPLE LACTOFERMENTO: Peel a pineapple and cut it into pieces. Place the fruit and the peel in a vacuum bag and add 20 grams (3½ teaspoons) salt, vacuum-seal it, and leave it in a dark, dry place at 82.4°F (28°C) for 4 to 6 days. Strain the mixture, bottle it, and refrigerate it.

CILANTRO AIR: Weigh and add 200 ml (7 oz.) water, 100 ml (3¼ oz.) simple syrup, 1.5 grams (¼ teaspoon) ascorbic acid, and 6 grams fresh cilantro leaves in a Thermomix and blend at 7.5 speed for 30 seconds (or use a blender or food processor). Then filter using a fine-mesh sieve. In a jug, add 3 grams (½ teaspoon) soy lecithin and incorporate the mixture with a hand blender for 60 seconds. Bottle it and refrigerate it.

MALAS DECISIONES

CABUYA ROOFTOP
AGUASCALIENTES 158 COL. CONDESA,
ALCALDÍA CUAUHTÉMOC

Making a spontaneous "bad decision" at an after-party, Rocco Luna created a cocktail using the eclectic mix of ingredients he had at home at the time: some fruits, juices, and a low-quality spirit. The morning after, he realized that it was indeed a *mala decision*. However, it was hard to deny the remarkably well-crafted flavor that had emerged—a refreshing, tropical symphony that enticed with every sip. Determined to refine his accidental masterpiece, Rocco replaced the lackluster spirit with a quality gin, ensured that only freshly squeezed juices were used, and introduced an array of fresh fruits to the mix. The result was nothing short of magical, so "'Never, but never . . . regret your bad decisions," as Rocco says.

GLASSWARE: Goblet

GARNISH: Cucumber slice; dehydrated pineapple or grapefruit

- 1 piece guava
- 1 piece cucumber
- 2 oz. | 60 ml gin
- 1 oz. | 30 ml pineapple juice
- ½ oz. | 15 ml fresh lemon juice
- ½ oz. | 15 ml simple syrup
- Ginger ale, to top

1. Place the guava, the cucumber, and the gin in a shaker and muddle. Fill the shaker with ice.

2. Add all the remaining ingredients, except the ginger ale, to the shaker.

3. Shake vigorously until chilled and strain the cocktail over ice cubes into a goblet.

4. Top with ginger ale and garnish with a cucumber slice and dehydrated pineapple or grapefruit.

ROSSO JAMAICA

CIENA
ALFONSO REYES 101, COL. CONDESA,
ALCALDÍA CUAUHTÉMOC

The magic of this mocktail lies in Runneght, a sustainable, alcohol-free distilled spirit infused with herbal ingredients, skillfully crafted by Fátima León and Fran Calvo. Drawing inspiration from the principles of Zero Waste, Karen Villagómez has ingeniously designed a beverage where each ingredient used is repurposed from the "waste" generated by other recipes at Ciena's bar, seamlessly integrated in a simple yet original way.

GLASSWARE: Rocks glass

GARNISH: Dehydrated Hibiscus Chips with Chili (see recipe)

- Sweet-and-Sour Hibiscus Salt (see recipe), for the rim
- 1½ oz. | 45 ml Runneght Rosso
- 1½ oz. | 45 ml Tepache (see recipe)
- ½ oz. | 15 ml Hibiscus Syrup (see recipe)
- ½ oz. | 15 ml fresh lime juice

1. Wet half of a rocks glass and dip it into the Sweet-and-Sour Hibiscus Salt.
2. Combine all of the ingredients in a cocktail shaker filled with ice.
3. Shake vigorously until chilled, then strain the mocktail over ice into the rocks glass.
4. Garnish with Dehydrated Hibiscus Chips with Chili.

SWEET-AND-SOUR HIBISCUS SALT: Finely grind the leftover dehydrated hibiscus chips together with chili powder. Once this is done, thoroughly combine it with 1 kilogram (2¼ pounds) sugar, 10 grams (2 teaspoons) Tajín, and 5 grams (1 teaspoon) citric acid.

TEPACHE: In a pot, add the peels from two pineapples, 1½ kilograms (54 oz.) piloncillo (unrefined cane sugar), 3 liters (4 cups) water, 15 grams (½ oz.) star anise, and 25 grams (about 4) cinnamon sticks. Bring the mixture to a boil. Remove from heat and let it cool. Once it's cool, cover the tepache with a cloth and allow it to ferment at room temperature for 3 days. After that, strain the mixture and allow it to continue fermenting in the refrigerator.

HIBISCUS SYRUP: In a pot, add 200 grams (7 oz.) dried hibiscus flowers, 1 kilogram (2¼ pounds) sugar, and 1½ liters (6 cups) water. Bring the mixture to a boil, allowing it to reduce until you achieve a syrup-like consistency. Let it cool, then strain the syrup. Reserve all the strained hibiscus flowers to make Dehydrated Hibiscus Chips with Chili.

DEHYDRATED HIBISCUS CHIPS WITH CHILI: Combine 200 grams (7 oz.) hibiscus flowers (which have been pre-infused in hibiscus syrup) with 100 grams (3½ oz.) sugar, 10 grams pink salt, 10 grams (2 teaspoons) Tajín, and 5 grams (1 teaspoon) citric acid. Mix thoroughly until the flowers are evenly coated. Proceed to dehydrate them in the oven at 158°F (70°C) for 5 hours or until the flowers are completely dry and crispy. Reserve some for the Sweet-and-Sour Hibiscus Salt.

DOS PARADAS

OSTRERÍA 109
AV. NUEVO LEÓN 109 COL. CONDESA,
ALCALDÍA CUAUHTÉMOC

José Raúl González Velasco, aka "Tosco," aims to break the formality by using innovative flavors such as corn silk or quelites, incorporating natural Mexican ingredients while emphasizing the importance of temporality and seasonality. Dos Paradas, a play on words, is a cocktail that combines the sweet and bitter, the fizziness and the tropical elements, creating a refreshing and perfect blend on your palate.

GLASSWARE: Wineglasses, chilled

- 2½ oz. | 75 ml Tropical Batch (see recipe)
- 1½ oz. | 45 ml vodka
- Dash simple syrup
- 2 oz. | 60 ml sparkling wine, chilled

1. Chill two wineglasses. Combine all of the ingredients, except the sparkling wine, in a cocktail shaker filled with ice.

2. Shake vigorously until chilled and strain the cocktail into a chilled wineglass.

3. Pour the chilled sparkling wine in another wineglass.

TROPICAL BATCH: Add 1 (750 ml) bottle sauvignon blanc, 500 ml (2 cups) passion fruit pulp, 500 ml (2 cups) piloncillo syrup, 500 ml (2 cups) Corn Silk Infusion (see recipe), and 4 dashes Angostura bitters in a container. Stir to combine.

CORN SILK INFUSION: Combine 500 ml (2 cups) water with 50 grams (2 oz.) corn silk in a saucepan. Bring it to a boil and cook for 4 minutes. Once it reaches room temperature, strain it, and reserve it for the Tropical Batch recipe.

MARÍA MEZCAL

TURKANA-HOTEL PARQUE MÉXICO
NUEVO LEÓN 100 COL. CONDESA
ALCALDÍA CUAUHTÉMOC

Turkana is characterized by its air of mysticism, exoticism, and eroticism as it evokes the essence of an old cabaret and an art gallery. These feelings are beautifully captured in this deconstructed cocktail crafted by Eduardo Alvarado.

GLASSWARE: Rocks glass, skull glass

GARNISH: Chicozapote & Orange Juice Pearls (see recipe)

- Hibiscus Salt, for the rim (see recipe)
- 2 oz. | 60 ml Vanilla-Infused Mezcal (see recipe), chilled
- 10 oz. | 300 ml Orange & Chicozapote Juice (see recipe)

1. Wet the rim of the skull glass and dip it into the Hibiscus Salt.

2. Pour the mezcal into the skull glass and the juice into a rocks glass filled with ice cubes.

3. Garnish with the pearls.

HIBISCUS SALT: Muddle ¼ cup dehydrated hibiscus flowers with ½ cup coarse sea salt until it's finely ground.

VANILLA-INFUSED MEZCAL: Add one vanilla pod to 1 (750 ml) bottle of mezcal. Let it rest for 48 hours. Strain it and keep it in the refrigerator.

ORANGE & CHICOZAPOTE JUICE: Extract fresh orange juice and blend it 4:1 with chicozapote. Strain it and reserve it.

CHICOZAPOTE & ORANGE JUICE PEARLS: Mix 1 gram sodium alginate with 200 ml (6¾ oz.) orange juice. Let it rest for 30 minutes and meanwhile mix 400 ml (13½ oz.) water with 4 grams calcium. Using a pipette, drop the mixture of orange juice into the calcium mixture. Let it rest for 2 minutes, stir with a perforated spoon, and rinse with water.

DELETED SOULS

DELETED SOULS COCKTAILTHEQUE
TAMAULIPAS 61C COL. CONDESA,
ALCALDÍA CUAUHTÉMOC

This is the liquid dream of Nur Farah Sojo and "Lwan" Luis Antonio Medina Salas. Crafted by Lwan, this drink represents the bar's originality.

GLASSWARE: Coupe glass

GARNISH: Dehydrated lemon wheel; smoked hickory and cinnamon

- 1½ oz. | 45 ml mezcal
- ½ oz. | 15 ml elderflower liqueur
- ¾ oz. | 22.5 ml fresh lemon juice
- ½ oz. | 15 ml grapefruit juice
- ½ oz. | 15 ml Cinnamon Syrup (see recipe)
- Pinch activated charcoal

1. Combine all of the ingredients in a cocktail shaker filled with ice.

2. Shake vigorously until chilled and double-strain the cocktail into a coupe.

3. Garnish with a dehydrated lemon and smoke the cocktail in a smoking dome with hickory wood chips and cinnamon.

CINNAMON SYRUP: Place 4 cinnamon sticks in 1 liter (4 cups) water and 1 kilogram (2¼ pounds) sugar in a saucepan. Bring the mixture to a boil, lower the heat, and reduce until syrupy. Strain and store the syrup.

ROSA SPRITZ

CONDESA DF
AVENIDA VERACRUZ 102, COL. CONDESA,
ALCALDÍA CUAUHTÉMOC

With an Italian influence, this fresh, fruity, and slightly bitter cocktail is ideal served as an aperitif.

GLASSWARE: Highball glass

GARNISH: Dehydrated strawberry, fresh basil leaves

- 2 oz. | 60 ml Cocchi Rosa
- 2 oz. | 60 ml prosecco
- Sparkling water, to top

1. Chill a highball glass. Build the cocktail over ice in the highball and stir softly until chilled.
2. Top with sparkling water.
3. Garnish with a dehydrated strawberry and fresh basil leaves.

NAMI SPRITZ

NAMI SAKE

Mexico doesn't only produce agave-based spirits. While traditionally associated with Japan, Nami Sake in Mexico has been crafted as a clash of two different cultures in Culiacán, Sinaloa. This is one of the most refreshing, easy-to-drink yet complex cocktails you're likely to try.

GLASSWARE: Highball glass

GARNISH: Orange twist

- 1 oz. | 30 ml Nami Sake
- ½ oz. | 15 ml Lillet Blanc
- 3 oz. | 90 ml aloe vera juice
- Sparkling water, to top

1. Build the cocktail in a highball containing ice cubes, adding ingredients in the order listed.
2. Stir softly to combine.
3. Garnish with an orange twist.

NUT FASHIONED

SOD

AMSTERDAM 53 COL. HIPÓDROMO CONDESA,
ALCALDÍA CUAUHTÉMOC

SOD, which means "secret" in Hebrew, is not just a bar; it's a mysterious experience that begins at an intriguing entrance, a place that will make you feel like you're in the tent of a powerful Bedouin sheik. Both the dishes from chef Daniel Ovadía and the magnificent cocktails created by Claudia Cabrera Rodríguez are inspired by the Bedouins and use Middle Eastern ingredients. This cocktail, a riff on the Old Fashioned, is smoked and served with a basket of phyllo pastry with creamy honey pistachio filling.

GLASSWARE: Rocks glass

GARNISH: Skeleton leaf, basket of phyllo pastry with creamy honey pistachio

---

- 1 sugar cube
- 3 drops Angostura bitters
- 2 oz. | 60 ml Fat-Washed Bourbon (see recipe)
- Coffee wood, to smoke

1. Place one sugar cube in a rocks glass and add the bitters.
2. Add the bourbon, then a large ice cube.
3. Stir until chilled.
4. Garnish with a skeleton leaf and a basket of phyllo pastry with creamy honey pistachio.
5. Using a smoking gun, or a heat-safe surface, cloche, and kitchen torch, smoke the cocktail with coffee wood.

FAT-WASHED BOURBON:

Clarify 300 grams (2¾ sticks) un-salted butter. Toast 200 grams (1 cup) pecan nuts in the butter and mix it with 100 grams (¾ cup) honey. Let the mixture cool to 104°F (40°C). Add 1 (750 ml) bottle of bourbon and transfer the mixture to a container with a lid. Store it in the freezer overnight. Break the butter layer and filter the bourbon through cheesecloth or a coffee filter.

CUAUHTÉMOC

JUINOTE

CONSERVATORIO

OTTER MELON

UN CANTARITO

GAIA

CLOVER TALL

Cuauhtémoc, which means "descending eagle," was the last Tlatoani or Aztec emperor of Tenochtitlán, who defended his people during the Spanish conquest. In his honor this neighborhood bears his name.

Here you can discover iconic landmarks like the Angel of Independence, also known as the Mexican victory symbol; the Castle of Chapultepec; and exclusive hotels like the St. Regis, which has a Greek-inspired restaurant, Mentor. You'll also find the tallest buildings of the city, which host incredible viewing spots, like Ling Ling; modern cantinas like Salón Ríos; and cozy neighborhood bars like Café Ocampo.

JUINOTE

CALAVERA MEXOLOGY

Have you ever imagined what Mexico would taste like if it were a drink? Raúl Ontiveros created Juinote, a cocktail that will introduce you to the ancestral liquid experience of Mexico where flavors merge with rich traditions and innovative mixology. Tejuino, the ancient beverage, is meticulously crafted using maize and piloncillo, with its cherished recipe passed down through generations.

GLASSWARE: Calavera clay cantarito

GARNISH: Cucumber slices, Yahualica chile

- Chamoy sauce, for the rim
- Tajín, for the rim
- 7 oz. | 210 ml tejuino
- 1 oz. | 30 ml fresh lemon juice
- 1 oz. | 30 ml tamarind paste
- Pink salt, to taste
- 7 oz. | 210 ml beer, to top

1. Wet the calavera clay cantarito with chamoy sauce and dip it into Tajín.
2. Combine all of the ingredients, except for the beer, in a cocktail shaker filled with ice.
3. Shake vigorously until chilled and strain the cocktail over ice cubes into the cantarito and top with beer.
4. Garnish with cucumber slices and a Yahualica chile.

CONSERVATORIO

CAFÉ OCAMPO
PLAZA MELCHOR OCAMPO 14, COL. CUAUHTÉMOC,
ALCALDÍA CUAUHTÉMOC

Nominated as the best new cocktail bar in 2019 by Tales of the Cocktail, Conservatorio is a cult-worthy bar. Get ready for a mind-blowing experience with this masterpiece crafted by Julio Delgado. It blends the rich heritage of Mexican spirits with the time-honored artistry of Italy.

GLASSWARE: Highball glass

GARNISH: Lemon twist, frozen strawberry

- 2 oz. | 60 ml yogurt
- 1½ oz. | 45 ml tequila
- 1 oz. | 30 ml bianco vermouth
- 1 oz. | 30 ml white crème de cacao
- ¾ oz. | 22.5 ml fresh lime juice

1. Combine all of the ingredients in a cocktail shaker filled with ice.
2. Shake vigorously until chilled.
3. Double-strain the cocktail into a highball glass.
4. Garnish with a lemon twist and a frozen strawberry.

OTTER MELON

PINK RAMBO
CALLE CEDRO 66 COLONIA SANTA MARÍA LA RIBERA,
ALCALDÍA CUAUHTÉMOC

Pink Rambo cocktails have a modern touch of techniques where fermentations, carbonations, infusions, and distillations play an important role. Crafted by Luca Simpson, and originally made with cachaça, mint, and Portuguese tomatoes, this Mexican version was part of BēVy on tour across different Mexican bars.

✳

GLASSWARE: Beaker

GARNISH: Pickled watermelon strip

- 2 oz. | 60 ml Watermelon Juice (see recipe)
- 1¾ oz. | 52.5 ml Koche el Mezcal Elemental
- 1¼ oz. | 37.5 ml water
- ½ oz. | 15 ml Tomatillo Water (see recipe)
- ½ oz. | 15 ml Ruda Syrup (see recipe)

1. Combine all of the ingredients in a container.
2. Chill the batch as close as you can to 30.2°F (-1°C)
3. Carbonate the mixture: use 4BAR/60 PSI and let rest in the refrigerator, or carbonate twice with a carbonation machine such as a Sodastream.
4. Pour into a beaker filled with ice.
5. Garnish with a pickled watermelon strip.

WATERMELON JUICE: Cut a watermelon into chunks, removing the seeds and rind. Blend the chunks and strain the mixture. Add 2% by weight malic and 4% citric acid. Let it rest in a refrigerator overnight in a covered jug. Separate the fibers using the siphon technique with a tube to flow from top to almost the bottom to clarify naturally with the help of gravity.

TOMATILLO WATER: Blend 3 parts tomatillos with 1 part water. Bring the mixture to a boil and strain the mixture through a coffee filter.

RUDA SYRUP: Sous vide–infuse ruda (an herb with tarragon-like characteristics) with simple syrup at 131°F (55°C).

UN CANTARITO

SALÓN RÍOS
RÍO NILO 71 COL. CUAUHTÉMOC,
ALCALDÍA CUAUHTÉMOC

The iconic Un Cantarito was designed by the 2018 World Class Champion Marco Dorantes as a twist on classic Jaliscan cantaritos, where the pineapple notes add freshness to the mix.

✳

GLASSWARE: Cantarito or clay cup
GARNISH: Grapefruit half-moon, lemon half-moon, lime half-moon

---

- Tajín, for the rim
- Salt, for the rim
- 2 oz. | 60 ml grapefruit soda
- 1½ oz. | 45 ml Tequila Altos Reposado
- 1½ oz. | 45 ml grapefruit juice
- ½ oz. | 15 ml pineapple juice
- ½ oz. | 15 ml fresh lime juice

1. Wet the rim of the cantarito or clay cup and dip it into Tajín and salt.
2. Combine all of the ingredients in a cocktail shaker filled with three ice cubes.
3. Shake vigorously until chilled.
4. Strain the cocktail into the cantarito or clay cup filled with ice cubes.
5. Garnish with grapefruit, lemon, and lime half-moons.

GAIA

The Bloody Mary remains the signature cocktail of the St. Regis, originally designed by Fernand Petiot in New York's King Cole Bar back in 1934. As the tradition continues, each St. Regis has its unique, locally inspired interpretation, and Mentor, a delightful Greek restaurant in St. Regis Mexico City, is no exception. Crafted by Enriko Pali, Gaia is a clarified Bloody Mary that incorporates tequila for a Mexican touch and Greek yogurt and Greek feta.

GLASSWARE: Highball glass

GARNISH: Cherry tomato, Kalamata olives

- 4 oz. Clarified Tomato Juice with Tequila, Greek Yogurt, and Feta Cheese (see recipe)

1. Add the ingredients to a highball containing one collins ice cube.

2. Stir until chilled.

3. Garnish with a cherry tomato and Kalamata olives.

CLARIFIED TOMATO JUICE WITH TEQUILA, GREEK YOGURT, AND FETA CHEESE: Add 1 (750 ml) bottle of tequila blanco, 1 liter (4 cups) milk, 1 kilogram (5 cups) Greek yogurt, 200 ml (6¾ oz.) lemon juice, 6 pieces of feta cheese, 10 pieces of different tomatoes, 1 peeled cucumber, 1 sliced green pepper, 1 sliced red pepper, 1 sliced jalapeño, and 1 sliced serrano pepper to a container and blend it. Refrigerate the mixture in a sealed container overnight. Use a super bag to strain and clarify the mixture.

CLOVER TALL

STEAK CLUB
AV. PASEO DE LA REFORMA 333,
ALCALDÍA CUAUHTÉMOC

The Angel of Independence holds a special place in the heart of both Mexicans and visitors. It's with this view that Steak Club, ranked 37 in the list of World's Best Steak Restaurants in 2022, reflects the vibrant energy of CDMX in its cocktails. Crafted by head mixologist Adrián Martínez, winner of first place in Legends of London in 2018, Clover Tall is a cocktail focused on sweet and floral notes with a familiar inspiration using a majestic crystalline ice cube.

GLASSWARE: Tall coupe glass

GARNISH: Crystalline ice cube

- 3 raspberry pieces
- 1⅕ oz. | 36 ml Beefeater Pink Strawberry Gin
- ¾ oz. | 22.5 ml fresh lime juice
- ½ oz. | 15 ml Chambord
- ½ oz. | 15 ml cranberry juice
- ½ oz. | 15 ml simple syrup
- ⅓ oz. | 10 ml aquafaba
- Culinary lavender extract, to aromatize

1. Add the raspberries to a cocktail shaker and muddle.
2. Add the remaining ingredients, except for the lavender, to the cocktail shaker and dry-shake vigorously.
3. Add ice cubes to the shaker and shake vigorously until chilled.

4. Double-strain the cocktail into a tall coupe filled with one perfect crystalline ice cube.

5. Perfume with culinary lavender extract.

JUÁREZ

TIBURÓN, TIBURÓN

HANSEL AND GRETEL

GARIBALDI (NA)

HUSMAN PORN STAR

NAKED AND DRUNK

ALMA CRISTALINA

JEKYLL AND HYDE

TIERRA ROJA

PISCOMELO

NEGRONI ORIGEN

GUANAMÉ CARAMEL CREAM

XIBALBA

This is one of the most eclectic and charming neighborhoods of the city, named after the former Mexican president Benito Juárez.

Juárez is a vibrant district where colorful murals, historical facades, galleries, and emerging establishments come together in a dynamic nightlife scene. Secret speakeasies, internationally renowned bars, mezcalerías, and outstanding gastronomy create the perfect space for trendsetters.

Colonia Juárez is the home to the third place–awarded bar, Handshake, in the World's 50 Best Bars, and of the iconic Fifty Mils.

TIBURÓN, TIBURÓN

CICATRIZ
DINAMARCA 44 COL. JUÁREZ, ALCALDÍA CUAUHTÉMOC

Founded by siblings Jake and Scarlett Linderman, Cicatriz is a place where small organic producers collaborate to craft interesting creations. In 2018, they earned a spot on *GQ* magazine's list of "The Best Bars in America," so get ready to enjoy this citrus delight cocktail with avocado notes.

GLASSWARE: Coupe glass

GARNISH: Orange peel twist

- 2 oz. | 60 ml Gin de Las Californias Cítrico
- 1 oz. | 30 ml orange juice
- ¾ oz. | 22.5 ml fresh lime juice

- ¾ oz. | 22.5 ml Avocado Leaf and Thyme Syrup (see recipe)
- 1 to 2 drops orange bitters

1. Combine all the ingredients in a cocktail shaker filled with ice.

2. Shake vigorously until chilled then double-strain the cocktail into a coupe.

3. Garnish with an orange peel twist.

AVOCADO LEAF AND THYME SYRUP: In a saucepan, combine 15 avocado leaves, 5 grams (1 teaspoon) thyme, approximately 5 bay leaves, 500 grams (2 cups) sugar, and 500 ml (2 cups) water. Bring the mixture to a boil for 3 to 5 minutes. Once cooled, strain the syrup to remove the leaves and herbs.

NICOLÁS CASTRO, FIFTY MILS

AV. PASEO DE LA REFORMA 500, COL. JUÁREZ, ALCALDÍA CUAUHTÉMOC

One of the most iconic mixology spots in Mexico City is the much-awarded Fifty Mils at the Four Seasons. With a seductive atmosphere, this urban oasis takes its name from the 50 ml (1¾ oz.) measure typically served in most classic and signature cocktails. Fifty Mils intertwines the use of local products with storytelling, between the staff and their guests, that resonates in every sip.

Nicolás Castro (@nikocastor), bar manager, brings his vast Latin American experience to the establishment. From Buenos Aires, Nicolás's journey through the world of mixology spans more than two decades. "My latest project there was managing the bar Frank's, the first in Argentina to enter the World's 50 Best Bars list in 2012 at number 36. In 2015, I had the opportunity to move to Quito, Ecuador, to manage a restaurant and open the city's first high-end cocktail bar. My next stop was Lima, Peru, where I opened my first bar, the city's only speakeasy, and a restaurant. After the pandemic, I decided to seize the opportunity to come to Mexico. In terms of competitions, I had won the Angostura Challenge in Argentina back in 2015 and in 2018, and the World Class Peru. In the global final in Berlin I placed fourteenth among the 57 competing countries."

Fifty Mils's current menu is themed "Fairy Drinks" and features a charmed collection of cocktails inspired by beloved characters such as Little Red Riding Hood, Hansel and Gretel, Cinderella, Snow White, Rumpelstiltskin, and Beauty and the Beast. For instance, Caperucita Roja (Little Red Riding Hood) integrates a blend of whiskey fat-washed with sausages, pear syrup, apple soda, goat cheese foam, and serrano ham—definitely a mix that would tempt the wolf's appetite.

Each one of them is pure magic that promises to enchant your evening!

HANSEL AND GRETEL

FIFTY MILS
AV. PASEO DE LA REFORMA 500, COL. JUÁREZ,
ALCALDÍA CUAUHTÉMOC

The Grimm Brothers' folk tale of Hansel and Gretel is the inspiration for this cocktail, which gives you a taste of each of the elements the witch gives the children, starting with vodka infused in gingerbread cookies, hazelnut liqueur, dried fruit liqueur, vanilla, almonds, and a sour touch accompanied by caramelized cocoa popcorn (pebbles), making this a journey of fantastic flavors. "The glass comes imprisoned in a cage, representing the place where the witch trapped Hansel," says bar manager Nicolás Castro. "The chocolate popcorn [symbolizes] the crumbs Hansel leaves in the forest to find his way home safely."

GLASSWARE: Rocks glass

- 1½ oz. | 45 ml Gingerbread Cookies–Infused Vodka (see recipe)
- 1½ oz. | 45 ml hazelnut liqueur
- ½ oz. | 15 ml dried fruit liqueur
- Vanilla extract, to taste
- Almonds, to taste
- Caramelized cocoa popcorn, to taste

1. Combine all the ingredients in a cocktail shaker with ice.

2. Shake vigorously until chilled.

3. Strain the cocktail into a rocks glass.

GINGERBREAD COOKIES INFUSED–VODKA: Add 200 grams gingerbread cookies to 1 (750 ml) bottle of vodka and steep for 24 hours. Strain before use.

GARIBALDI (NA)

HANDSHAKE
AMBERES 65, COL. JUÁREZ, ALCALDÍA CUAUHTÉMOC

A speakeasy ranked number 3 on the World's 50 Best Bars 2023, and number 2 on the list of North America's 50 Best Bars in 2023, Handshake is where the passion for mixology transforms into cocktail masterpieces. Eric van Beek designed Garibaldi as a nonalcoholic option—using a fancy rotary evaporator—that doesn't sacrifice an extraordinary liquid experience. By skipping the evaporation, you can make the regular version of it as well.

GLASSWARE: Collins glass
GARNISH: Orange wheel

- 3 oz. | 90 ml Fluffy Orange Juice Foam (see recipe)
- 1½ oz. | 45 ml Bitter Di Battista 0.0 (see recipe)
- Dash saline solution

1. Build the cocktail, in the order of the ingredients listed, in a collins glass containing a crystal-clear ice stick.
2. Stir to combine.

BITTER DI BATTISTA 0.0: Place Bitter Di Battista, as needed, in a rotary evaporator to extract the alcohol.

FLUFFY ORANGE JUICE FOAM: Combine 2 cups orange juice and ¼ cup sugar in a container and mix until the sugar is dissolved. Pour the mixture into a cream whipper. Charge the cream whipper with a cartridge and shake well before using.

HUSMAN PORN STAR

HUSMAN BISTRO
PRAGA 29, COL. JUÁREZ, ALCALDÍA CUAUHTÉMOC

Inspired by Douglas Ankrah's classic recipe, this cocktail is a modern twist on the Porn Star Martini. It aims to awaken sensuality and curiosity, evolving into a seduction story. Vodka is replaced by sotol and, with the "milk punch" technique, it becomes an immersive experience.

GLASSWARE: Coupe glass

GARNISH: Passion fruit gummy

- 1½ oz. | 45 ml Vanilla-Infused Sotol (see recipe)
- 1½ oz. | 45 ml passion fruit pulp
- ½ oz. | 15 ml mango liqueur
- ½ oz. | 15 ml vanilla syrup
- ½ oz. | 15 ml fresh lime juice
- Whole milk, as needed
- 1 oz. | 30 ml sparkling wine, to top

1. Chill a coupe. Combine all of the ingredients, except for the sparkling wine, in a container and let it rest for 2 hours.
2. Strain the "milk punch" until it has the desired clearness.
3. Pour the punch into a mixing glass filled with ice.
4. Stir until chilled then strain the cocktail into the chilled coupe.
5. Top with sparkling wine and garnish with a passion fruit gummy.

VANILLA-INFUSED SOTOL: Vacuum-seal one vanilla pod per liter Los Magos Sotol Blanco. Sous vide at 158°F (70°C) for 2 hours. Strain before use.

NAKED AND DRUNK

Elías Pablo Ahuejote uses Asian elements to craft, in liquid notes, the sensation of getting a kiss from someone you love. The result is a mystical cocktail, semisweet but with intense flavor.

GLASSWARE: Coupe glass

GARNISH: Freeze-dried pineapple inside a wooden cone

- 1½ oz. | 45 ml Creyente Mezcal
- 1 oz. | 30 ml Aperol
- 1 oz. | 30 ml pineapple juice
- ½ oz. | 15 ml simple syrup
- ½ oz. | 15 ml Honey Mango Yuzu (see recipe)

1. Chill a coupe glass. Combine all of the ingredients in a cocktail shaker filled with ice.
2. Shake vigorously until chilled, then strain the cocktail into the chilled coupe.
3. Garnish with freeze-dried pineapple inside a wooden cone.

HONEY MANGO YUZU: In a medium saucepan over medium heat, add 400 grams (about 1½ cups) mango puree, 250 grams (¾ cup) honey, 250 ml (about 1 cup) yuzu, and 500 ml (2 cups) water. Bring the mixture to a boil and boil for 5 minutes. Allow the mixture to cool, then strain, label, and refrigerate it.

ALMA CRISTALINA

PARKER & LENOX
GENERAL PRIM 100 COL. JUÁREZ,
ALCALDÍA CUAUHTÉMOC

Drinks tell a story, evoke memories of a person, or even call to mind a song. At Parker & Lenox, Alison Cruz crafted a cocktail that pairs harmoniously with jazz music in the background, where seven souls come together to tell a story. This one is the crystalline soul.

GLASSWARE: Rocks glass

GARNISH: None

- Dehydrated Serrano Pepper Salt (see recipe), for the rim

- 2 oz. | 60 ml Mezcal Señor de las Almas

- 2 oz. | 60 ml Passion Fruit Cordial (see recipe)

- ½ oz. | 15 ml fresh lime juice

- 1 oz. | 30 ml simple syrup

1. Wet the rim of the rocks glass and dip it into the serrano pepper salt.

2. Combine all of the ingredients in a cocktail shaker filled with ice.

3. Shake vigorously until chilled and strain the cocktail into a rocks glass filled with three ice cubes.

PASSION FRUIT CORDIAL: Add 500 ml (2 cups) passion fruit pulp, 150 ml (⅔ cup) water, and 300 grams (1½ cups) sugar to a blender and blend.

DEHYDRATED SERRANO PEPPER SALT: Cut 1 kilogram (about 2 pounds) serrano chiles in halves and remove the seeds. Place them in the oven for 12 hours at 176°F (80°C). Once they are golden, blend them together with Colima salt and malic acid, as needed.

JEKYLL AND HYDE

TOLEDO ROOFTOP
AV. CHAPULTEPEC 461 COL. JUÁREZ,
ALCALDÍA CUAUHTÉMOC

Like the novel, this cocktail contains a duality. In this case, the opposite ingredients complement each other to achieve balance. The tropical notes balance the mezcal's complexity and the celery encapsulates a sweet, sour, salty, and bitter experience in every sip.

GLASSWARE: Rocks glass

GARNISH: Fresh celery leaves, cucumber slice roll-up

- **Celery Salt (see recipe), for the rim**
- **2 oz. | 60 ml mezcal**

- **1 oz. | 30 ml Passion Fruit Concentrate (see recipe)**
- **1 oz. | 30 ml Pineapple Syrup (see recipe)**

1. Wet the rim of a rocks glass and dip it into the Celery Salt.

2. Add the remaining ingredients to a cocktail shaker filled with ice.

3. Shake vigorously until chilled.

4. Strain the cocktail over ice into the rocks glass.

5. Garnish with fresh celery leaves and a cucumber slice roll-up.

PASSION FRUIT CONCENTRATE: Extract the pulp of 1 passion fruit, remove the seeds, and strain it through a fine-mesh strainer.

PINEAPPLE SYRUP: Extract pineapple pulp (from 1 pineapple) then blend and strain the pulp through a fine-mesh strainer. Add an equal volume of sugar and cook the mixture over low heat until the syrup is reduced.

CELERY SALT: Add celery leaves and stalks from 1 head of celery to boiling water, then rapidly cool it in an ice water bath. Dehydrate the celery and grind it with Maldon sea salt.

TIERRA ROJA

XUNI MEZCALERÍA
LONDRES 178 COL. JUÁREZ,
ALCALDÍA CUAUHTÉMOC

Xuni Mezcalería is likely to be the only place in Mexico City that uses *colonche*, a fermented beverage made from the juice of tunas (the fruits of the prickly pear cactus), as a cocktail ingredient.

---
*

GLASSWARE: Rocks glass

GARNISH: Fresh epazote leaves, smoked cinnamon

- 2 oz. | 60 ml sotol
- 2 oz. | 60 ml Colonche (see recipe)
- ½ oz. | 15 ml fresh lime juice
- ½ oz. | 15 ml Nixta Licor de Elote
- ⅓ oz. | 10 ml epazote liqueur
- Dash simple syrup

1. Combine all of the ingredients in a cocktail shaker filled with ice.

2. Shake vigorously until chilled.

3. Strain the cocktail over ice into a rocks glass.

4. Garnish with fresh epazote leaves and smoked cinnamon.

COLONCHE: Extract the juice from the tunas (or red prickly pear cactus) and ferment it with Red Star Montrachet Yeast. Adjust the pH to 3.5 and 20 degrees Brix. Let the juice mature for 3 months before bottling. (This fermentation should ideally be done by an experienced professional.)

INGRID SOLÍS RODRÍGUEZ, LAS ESPIRITUOSAS

With over twenty-five years in the industry, Ingrid Solís Rodríguez's interest in Mexican spirits began casually when she got involved in the Taller Astrafilia, a cooperative project born in 2015 driven by appreciation of Mexico's biodiversity and the desire to produce artisanal beverages of the highest quality. Since then, as a Spaniard, she has fallen in love with Mexico's cultural diversity expressed through all the plants, roots, flowers, and landscapes found in the Aztec country.

The spirits that Ingrid—aka Chanchi—and her team craft are made exclusively from pesticide-free native Mexican plants and corn-based alcohol that highlights Mexico's authenticity. As of today, Las Espirituosas is a mostly female powerhouse that distributes four gins, four liqueurs, and four bitters. Its main goal is to support small brands and to create a network of places that support their use in bars. Each one of these products represents a fundamental part of Mexico's history.

For example, Cempasuchitl Liqueur is crafted from the iconic orange-colored flower used to decorate the graves and altars during the celebration of the Day of the Dead. The Axiote Liqueur has refreshing and aromatic notes that evoke Yucatan's gastronomy, such as the cochinita pibil. Their gins express a wide range of aromas, infused with thirty native botanicals. Other spirits, such as the corn-based whiskey, Astro, and raicilla from Jalisco contribute to Mexico's liquid heritage.

In the desert landscape of Sonora, the bacanora from Santo Cuviso emerges as a regional treasure. The artistry of distilled pulque and the authenticity of pox from Chiapas continue to be part of Mexican culture and history. Even rums, crafted from sugarcane, express the essence of Oaxaca and Morelia.

Las Espirituosas developed a liqueur for March 8—International Women's Day—as a symbol of unity, mutual support, and collaboration. This liqueur serves as a meaningful reminder that gender inequality is still a reality in 2024, and the proceeds will be donated to a women's shelter.

Therefore, this is a space for recognition of bartenders Alejandra S. Reynoso, Alexia Jiménez, Amalia Ramírez, Annais González, Claudia López, Dalia Martínez, Daniela Negrete, Gabriela López, Gisela Gracia, Giselle Bustamante, Isabel Ortega, Jacomine Flores, Jennifer Solís, Jessica Flores, Jimena Alva, Karla Valdés, Laura Jardon, María Orozco, Maria Molano, Mariana Zapata, Pam Martínez, Paula Campos, Sandra Maya, Yuranzi del Valle Silva, Valeria Flores, Victoria López, and all those who choose wisely which spirits they support in order to give wings to dreams and projects like Las Espirituosas.

PISCOMELO

VELVET SODA
CALLE DE DURANGO 272A, ROMA NORTE,
CUAUHTÉMOC

This sophisticated twist on the classic Peruvian Greyhound high-lights the citrus flavors of pisco and the refreshing essence from both red and white pomelo varieties from Michoacán, México.

* * *

GLASSWARE: Rocks glass

GARNISH: Grapefruit peel

- 3 grapefruits, supremed
- 2 lemon wedges
- 1 oz. | 30 ml Rompe Mar Pisco
- ½ oz. | 15 ml Agave Nectar Traficante
- Velvet Soda Pomelo, to top

1. Place the grapefruit and lemon wedges into a rocks glass and muddle them well.

2. Build the cocktail over ice in the glass and stir until chilled.

3. Top with the soda.

4. Garnish with a grapefruit peel.

NEGRONI ORIGEN

SOTOL FLOR DEL DESIERTO

Sotol is distilled from the *Dasylirion* genus of plants, commonly known as *sereque*, which was used in rituals and religious ceremonies in both the pre-Hispanic and Hispanic eras in the desert states of Chihuahua, Durango, and Coahuila. Despite the region where it's produced or the distillation process, sotols often have common characteristics—earthy undertones, green or vegetal qualities, and herbal, floral, and citrus aromas. Crafted by Oscar Olvera, this cocktail is a Chihuahuan version of a classic Negroni made with a vermouth made from Chihuahua Pinesque 5 Red Wine, which is fortified with Sotol Flor del Desierto and Chihuahuan mountain botanicals.

GLASSWARE: Rocks glass

GARNISH: Orange twist

- 1 oz. | 30 ml Flor del Desierto Sotol
- 1 oz. | 30 ml Campari
- 1 oz. | 30 ml Vermut Origen
- Orange peel, to express

1. Add the sotol, Campari, and vermouth to a rocks glass containing 1 ice cube.
2. Stir gently to combine.
3. Express an orange peel over the drink and discard the peel. Garnish with an orange twist

GUANAMÉ CARAMEL CREAM

GUANAMÉ
CARRETERA A MÉXICO 11700, LA PILA,
SAN LUIS POTOSÍ

Each sip is a delightful and silky caramel sensation; this cocktail is crafted to enjoy those unique sweet moments of life. If you can get ahold of Dondé Coco Nieve wafer cookies, that's the best way to finish this preparation.

GLASSWARE: Coupette glass

GARNISH: Frozen raspberry skewer, vanilla wafer cookie

- 1½ oz. | 45 ml Guanamé Caramel Cream
- 1 oz. | 30 ml espresso
- ½ oz. | 30 ml Beefeater Blackberry Gin
- ½ oz. | 30 ml Frangelico

1. Chill a coupette glass. Combine all of the ingredients in a cocktail shaker filled with ice.

2. Shake vigorously until chilled.

3. Double-strain the cocktail into the coupette.

4. Garnish with a frozen raspberry skewer and a vanilla wafer cookie.

XIBALBA

SONORA GRILL
PASEO DE LA REFORMA NTE. I COL. TABACALERA,
ALCALDÍA CUAUHTÉMOC

Adrián Martínez not only made it to the final 50 bartenders in the Hennessy My Way competition in 2023, he also won second place in Patrón's 2019 Margarita of the Year competition. At Sonora Grill, he focuses on mixology that pays tribute to Mexican culture, a prime example being this cocktail inspired by the mysterious Mayan underworld, Xibalba.

GLASSWARE: Skull mug

GARNISH: Mango half-moons, edible flowers

- 2¾ oz. | 82.5 ml Cacao-Infused Mango (see recipe)
- 1½ oz. | 45 ml Patrón Reposado Tequila
- ¾ oz. | 22.5 ml agave nectar
- ½ oz. | 15 ml Nixta Licor de Elote
- ½ oz. | 15 ml lime juice

1. Combine all of the ingredients in a cocktail shaker filled completely with ice.
2. Shake vigorously until chilled, then dirty-pour (don't strain) the cocktail over ice into a skull mug.
3. Add crushed ice to top and garnish with mango half-moons and edible flowers.

CACAO-INFUSED MANGO: Add 34 oz. natural mango extract and 20¼ oz. cocoa to a bowl and mix thoroughly. Transfer the mixture to a 1-liter bottle and let it cool in the refrigerator for 6 hours.

POLANCO AND
LAS LOMAS

PINEAPPLE DREAM	MARGARITA YUZU KOSHO
MAYAHUEL	NANCHE MARTINI
BLACK MARTINI	TOKOYA MARGARITA
LA SIRENA	YUZU KOSHO
NEGRONI PIAMONTE	MICTLÁN
YAKUSA	VERDE MARÍA
AUTORETRATO	NUBE
COMETA	SOL NACIENTE
MARGARITA CON REVOLUCIÓN	LEMON CHEESECAKE
POSEIDON	GREEN SUIT
FUGU	VERDE VIDA
TIPSY PARROT	FIGLET
BLACKBERRY 75	ALMA FINCA WHITE LADY
MARGARITA CADILLAC	ATACAMA SUNSET

Polanco and Las Lomas are synonymous with luxury, elegance, and sophistication. From the most exclusive boutique stores to the most Instagrammable neon sign in the city—"México mi amor"— and the lush greenery of Parque Lincoln, Polanco, especially "Polanquito," offers trendy, classic, and innovative culinary and mixology masterpieces.

This is a district to celebrate life and cultural diversity, to savor cochinita pibil tacos standing up, and to enjoy a fine dining experience at one of the world's best restaurants. It's also a place to experience memorable cocktails, of course.

PINEAPPLE DREAM

AMARAL
CAMPOS ELÍSEOS 218, COL. POLANCO,
ALCALDÍA MIGUEL HIDALGO

Get ready to be part of a one-of-a-kind adventure with this mixology masterpiece. This blend is a perfect combination of the Mexican essence, where the harmonious union of pepper and tequila creates a sensory journey like no other. Controy is a Mexican-made triple sec.

GLASSWARE: Rocks glass

GARNISH: Pineapple leaves held with a copper toothpick

- Agave nectar, for the rim, plus ½ oz. | 15 ml
- Black salt, for the rim
- 10 cilantro leaves
- 2 oz. | 60 ml Cascahuín Extra Añejo Tequila
- ½ oz. | 15 ml Controy
- ½ oz. | 15 ml fresh Eureka lemon juice
- 4 drops black habanero chili sauce

1. Wet the rim of a rocks glass with the agave nectar and dip it into the black salt.
2. Place the cilantro leaves in a cocktail shaker and muddle.
3. Add the remaining ingredients to the shaker with ice and shake vigorously until chilled.

4. Strain the cocktail into the rocks glass filled with a gourmet ice cube deco-
rated with different patterns.

5. Garnish with three pineapple leaves held with a copper toothpick.

MAYAHUEL

BEEFBAR
MARIANO ESCOBEDO 700 COL. NUEVA ANZURES,
ALCALDÍA MIGUEL HIDALGO

BeefBar Mexico opened its doors on August 11, 2014. To mark its grand opening, Mayahuel was crafted. Inspired by the goddess of agave, it infuses a Mexican identity and flair into a venue concept that was imported from Monaco.

GLASSWARE: Martini glass

GARNISH: Dehydrated pineapple slice

- **Worm salt, for the rim**
- **2 oz. | 60 ml mezcal**
- **1 oz. | 30 ml passion fruit liqueur**
- **1 oz. | 30 ml orange juice**
- **1 oz. | 30 ml blue curaçao**
- **¼ oz. | 7.5 ml Passion Fruit Pulp (see recipe)**

1. Wet the rim of a martini glass and dip it into the worm salt.
2. Add the remaining ingredients to a cocktail shaker filled with ice.
3. Shake vigorously until chilled.
4. Strain the cocktail into the martini glass.
5. Garnish with a dehydrated pineapple slice.

PASSION FRUIT PULP: Select passion fruits with wrinkled skins for optimal sweetness. Cut them in half and scoop out the pulp, then place the pulp in a blender or food processor. Pulse. Strain the mixture through a fine-mesh strainer, discarding the seeds.

BLACK MARTINI

BLUE BAR

MARIANO ESCOBEDO 700, COL. NUEVA ANZURES,
ALCALDÍA MIGUEL HIDALGO

When art, style, and the finest mixology experts come together, the result can only be truly impressive. The Black Martini is an original creation in which activated charcoal is used to provide an unusual texture and visual presentation, and it also adds a black color and a slightly smoky flavor to the cocktail. Get ready for an unparalleled sensory experience.

GLASSWARE: Martini glass

GARNISH: Filthy Berries, lemon twist

- Chile piquín, for the side rim
- 2½ oz. | 75 ml pineapple juice
- 2 oz. | 60 ml gin
- 1 oz. | 30 ml fresh lemon juice
- 1 oz. | 30 ml Passion Fruit Syrup (see recipe)
- ½ oz. | 15 ml agave nectar
- 5 grams activated charcoal

1. Chill a martini glass. Wet one side of the martini glass rim and dip it into the chile piquín.
2. Add the remaining ingredients to a cocktail shaker filled with ice.
3. Shake vigorously until chilled.
4. Double-strain the cocktail into the chilled martini glass.
5. Garnish with Filthy Berries and a lemon twist.

PASSION FRUIT SYRUP: Add an equal amount of granulated sugar to the strained Passion Fruit Pulp (1 cup sugar for 1 cup pulp)—see page 141.

LA SIRENA

CAMPOMAR
AV. PRESIDENTE MASARYK 264, POLANCO IV SECC,
MIGUEL HIDALGO

Also known as "The Mermaid," La Sirena symbolizes the essence of the *vampirito*, a beloved Mexican beverage, but in the Campomar style. This artisanal creation offers a revitalizing blend of fruit juices with a zesty kick, capturing the classic Jaliscan flavor combination of tequila and chili.

GLASSWARE: Mermaid mug

GARNISH: Dehydrated orange supremes, banana leaf

- 3 oz. | 90 ml Chili Syrup (see recipe)
- 2 oz. | 60 ml tequila
- 1 oz. | 30 ml fresh lime juice

1. Combine all of the ingredients in a cocktail shaker filled with ice.

2. Shake vigorously until chilled then pour the cocktail into a mermaid mug.

3. Add crushed ice.

4. Garnish with dehydrated orange supremes and a banana leaf.

CHILI SYRUP: Add water, chiles de árbol, cascabel chiles, and mirasol chiles to a pot and heat until the peppers soften. Once they are soft, remove them and muddle them. Then, return them to the pot, adding sugar and hibiscus. Bring the mixture to a boil then allow it to cool. Strain the syrup before use.

FRANCISCO ORTEGA, BAGATELLE

TENNYSON 117 COL. POLANCO IV SECC, ALCALDÍA MIGUEL HIDALGO

In the heart of Mexico City, Bagatelle emerges as a vibrant oasis where French-Mediterranean culinary experience converges with the art of mixology as practiced by the talented Francisco Ortega. With a passion for flavors and a desire to explore the endless spectrum of sensations offered by meticulously crafted cocktails, Francisco has been at the forefront of Mexico City's dynamic cocktail scene, witnessing its remarkable transformation in recent years.

As head bartender at Bagatelle, Francisco's approach to mixology can be best described as a harmonious fusion of classic cocktails with local twists. He uses ingredients such as truffles, yuzu, and other exotic elements to blend tradition and innovation. His profound appreciation for Mexican spirits is evident through the offering of premium mezcal, tequila, and raicilla.

Francisco's creativity shines through in the seasonal and holiday -inspired cocktails. For instance, on Mexico's Independence Day, he designed a cocktail inspired by *chile en nogada*, a traditional Mexican dish synonymous with the celebration of September 16—a work of art, featuring pomegranate foam and tequila infused with the bold flavors of jalapeño and poblano peppers.

NEGRONI PIAMONTE

BAGATELLE
TENNYSON 117 COL. POLANCO IV SECC,
ALCALDÍA MIGUEL HIDALGO

Sophistication awaits you in this cocktail, where a symphony of flavors will undoubtedly elevate your cocktail experience to new heights. Cheers to the extraordinary!

GLASSWARE: Rocks glass

GARNISH: Skewer of seasonal black truffle, sun-dried cherry tomatoes, creamy buffalo mozzarella, and sprig of fresh basil

---

- 1 oz. | 30 ml Truffle-Washed Gin (see recipe)
- 1 oz. | 30 ml Carpano Antica Formula Vermouth
- 1 oz. | 30 ml Campari

1. Combine all of the ingredients in a mixing glass filled with 5 or 6 gourmet ice cubes.
2. Stir for 20 seconds until chilled.
3. Double-strain the cocktail into a rocks glass with 3 gourmet ice cubes.
4. Garnish with a skewer of seasonal black truffle, sun-dried cherry tomatoes, creamy buffalo mozzarella, and a sprig of fresh basil.

TRUFFLE-WASHED GIN: Muddle fresh black truffle, to taste, with 250 ml (1 cup) gin and 1 to 2 tablespoons high-quality white truffle oil in a glass jar. Allow the infusion to sit in a cool, dark place for 24 hours. Strain, refrigerate, and reserve the gin.

YAKUSA

COLMILLO

ARISTÓTELES 124 COL. POLANCO IV SECTOR,
ALCALDÍA MIGUEL HIDALGO

Fresh, with a sweet touch, this signature cocktail mixes green tea with mezcal, agave, and ginger ale—not to be missed!

GLASSWARE: Tiki owl mug

GARNISH: Basil, 3 pieces of guayaba

- ½ piece guayaba
- ½ oz. | 15 ml fresh lemon juice
- 1 oz. | 30 ml agave nectar

- 2 oz. | 60 ml green tea, cooled
- 2 oz. | 60 ml ginger ale
- 1½ oz. | 45 ml mezcal

1. Add the guayaba to a tiki mug and muddle with the lemon juice and agave nectar.
2. Add crushed ice.
3. Add the remaining ingredients and stir to combine.
4. Add a bit more crushed ice.
5. Garnish with a sprig of basil and 3 pieces of guayaba.

PAULA GARCÍA, BARRA MÉXICO

When it comes to the Mexican cocktail scene, Barra México is *the* event not to be missed!

Almost a decade ago, Barra México (barramexico.com; #thebarof thefuture) was born from the vision of Ara Carvallo and Paula García to promote the rise of Mexico's unique spirits, local talents, and vibrant bar culture across the world. It has shown not only the country's rich and modern identity by bridging education, promotion, and networking, but has also been empowering the women within the industry, according to Paula García. "It's something that has changed and evolved in very few years," she says. "I feel fortunate to have the opportunity to see the spaces and paths that have opened up for women, but there is still a long way to go."

Today, there are very few bartenders who don't keep Mexican spirits behind the bar. "In Mexico, we have found our way to create a mixology identity as a country: Mexican cocktails are traveling the world, classics like the Paloma and Margarita are regaining popularity, and traditional drinks are prepared with Mexican products," Paula says. "Bartenders are becoming more knowledgeable and seeking to learn more about Mexico and its regions. I see a lot of pride in working with local spirits, presenting Mexico to visitors, and bartenders aiming to specialize and talk more about the country, both domestically and internationally."

Barra México is beyond being a cocktail event. "We're proud to be the first event certified as carbon neutral and, last year, as climate positive," Paula says. "We follow a culture of peace, pay attention to inclusion, respect for others, gender equity, and contribute what we can to the planet. We couldn't create such a platform without doing something for the community we belong to and the world we live in."

AUTORETRATO

DIEGO Y YO
PRESIDENTE MASARYK 123, POLANCO,
ALCALDÍA MIGUEL HIDALGO

Get ready to sip to the memories of Diego Rivera and Frida Kahlo with Autoretrato, a cocktail that serves as a flavorful canvas, echoing Frida's words: "I paint myself because I am the one I know best." Raise your glass and toast to art, love, and Mexican cocktails!

GLASSWARE: Coupe glass
GARNISH: Edible rice paper printed with Frida's self-portrait

---

- 1 oz. | 30 ml pisco
- 1 oz. | 30 ml amaretto
- 1 oz. | 30 ml Passion Fruit Pulp (see recipe on page 141)
- 1 oz. | 30 ml fresh lemon juice syrup
- 1 oz. | 30 ml agave nectar
- 1 oz. | 30 ml egg white

1. Chill a coupe glass. Combine all of the ingredients in a cocktail shaker filled with ice.

2. Shake vigorously until chilled.

3. Strain the cocktail into the chilled coupe.

4. Garnish with an edible rice paper printed with Frida's self-portrait.

COMETA

DRYNK INC.
ANDRÉS BELLO 10, POLANCO IV SECC,
ALCALDÍA MIGUEL HIDALGO

Nothing is prettier than a Pacific Mexican sunset, especially in Punta Cometa, Oaxaca, a magical place where the sun kisses the horizon with an unmatched beauty. Just like this pink masterpiece, refreshing and intricate, that captures the essence of those serene moments.

GLASSWARE: Rocks glass

GARNISH: Banana leaves, pink baby rose

- 1½ oz. | 45 ml mezcal
- 1½ oz. | 45 ml pink guava juice
- ½ oz. | 15 ml Yellow Chartreuse
- ½ oz. | 15 ml fino sherry
- ½ oz. | 15 ml agave nectar
- ½ oz. | 15 ml fresh lemon juice
- Soda water, to top

1. Combine all of the ingredients, except for the soda water, in a cocktail shaker filled with ice.
2. Shake vigorously until chilled.
3. Strain the cocktail over ice into a rocks glass and top with soda.
4. Garnish with banana leaves and a pink baby rose.

MARGARITA CON REVOLUCIÓN

HACIENDA DE LOS MORALES
JUAN VÁZQUEZ DE MELLA 525, COL. POLANCO,
ALCALDÍA MIGUEL HIDALGO

This place crafts more than 1,500 margaritas per month (on the rocks, frozen, or frappé) using a diverse range of fruits such as mango, strawberry, passion fruit, tamarind, hibiscus, or the classic lime. Rim options are also available; you can choose from sea salt, worm salt, chili, or even blue tortilla salt.

GLASSWARE: Margarita glass

- Blue Tortilla Salt (see recipe), for the rim
- 12 oz. | 360 ml ice
- 2 oz. | 60 ml Tequila Revolución Añejo
- 1 oz. | 30 ml Casa D'Aristi Narano Bitter Orange Liqueur
- 1 oz. | 30 ml simple syrup
- 1 oz. | 30 ml fresh lime juice

1. Wet the rim of a margarita glass and dip it into the Blue Tortilla Salt.

2. Add all of the ingredients to a blender to combine.

3. Strain the mixture into the glass.

BLUE TORTILLA SALT: Combine equal parts toasted-but-not-burned blue tortilla with sea salt in a mortar and pestle and muddle until finely ground.

TANIA ALVARADO, EVEREST WINE AND SPIRITS

Tell us about your trajectory. How did your interest in the world of wines and spirits begin?

My joy and passion for gastronomy and the world around it started when I was at college, studying gastronomy and culinary arts. During my time in the restaurant industry, I was making experiences for luxury spirits brands like Johnnie Walker, Zacapa, and Buchanan´s, pairing dinners with different wineries and importers. Then I joined Ferrer and Associates to become public relations manager of Everest Wines and Spirits, an importer and distributor with a portfolio of more than 1,500 distinct labels from ten countries.

Which is your drink of choice? And why?

Ultimately a Hugo Spritz. It has the floral notes of St-Germain Elder-flower Liqueur that I like because they are subtle, it has bubbles that are always welcome, and a coolness that is a great option for a drink served as an aperitivo or at the end of a meal.

As an expert in brand building, can you share some examples in which you have contributed to the success of a brand?

In the last two years my focus in the cocktail industry is incorporating a drink with a fine tradition like port and using it in mixology, which has really been a challenge, to transform the dignity of this fortified wine and use it in bars, where it has a tremendous potential because, in a single product, it has flavor, sweetness, and strength.

Tell us about a memorable mixology experience that happened to you.

At the Royal Port Competition 2023, where more than forty bartend-ers from all of Mexico competed with original recipes where the main ingredient was port: during the final I presented before the ownership of the winery, chefs, and the media.

How do you see the cocktail scene in Mexico? How has it evolved? How has it served as a platform for boosting and introducing new products?

It has had exponential growth the last few years. We have bars in Mexico recognized as world class, where the creativity in flavors, presentation, and service every day becomes an unforgettable experience for the consumer, while also becoming increasingly challenging, where the challenge for the mixologist is to come up with ideas that increasingly take risks, creating opportunities for innovative products or products that were once totally outside the cocktail scene.

POSEIDON

CANTINA EL PALACIO
MOLIERE 222 COL. POLANCO,
ALCALDÍA MIGUEL HIDALGO

Just one sip and Poseidon will take you on a journey to the Mediterranean Sea by way of the Gulf of Mexico, with a gentle coconut breeze complemented by the Kypros Tequila and fresh thyme. This exquisite cocktail is the creation of Cesar Ponce-Burrin, the cofounder and global brand ambassador of Kypros Tequila.

GLASSWARE: Globe glass

GARNISH: Pineapple wedge, sprig of fresh thyme

- 1½ oz. | 45 ml Tequila Kypros Reposado
- 1 oz. | 30 ml Malibu Original
- 2 oz. | 60 ml fresh coconut water
- Sparkling water, to top

1. Chill a globe glass. Build the cocktail in the chilled globe glass over ice, slowly adding the ingredients in order, except for the sparkling water, which you slowly add through a barspoon.

2. Top with sparkling water and garnish with a pineapple wedge and sprig of fresh thyme.

FUGU

It is believed that seeing a Takifugu, or fugu, also known as a puffer fish, brings good luck. Now it's your turn to close your eyes, make a wish, and write it down—such is the experience you'll have when you try this cocktail from the team at La Buena Barra.

GLASSWARE: Puffer fish glass

GARNISH: Dehydrated citrus

- 2 oz. | 60 ml Matusalem Rum Clásico
- 2 oz. | 60 ml orange juice
- 1 oz. | 30 ml fresh seasonal fruit pulp
- ½ oz. | 15 ml simple syrup

1. Combine all of the ingredients in a cocktail shaker filled with ice.
2. Shake vigorously until chilled then strain over ice into a puffer fish glass.
3. Garnish with dehydrated citrus.

TIPSY PARROT

LA BUENA BARRA
ARISTÓTELES 124 COL. POLANCO,
ALCALDÍA MIGUEL HIDALGO

Picture yourself on a sun-kissed Mexican beach, with palm trees overhead, and the DJ playing the perfect song as you enjoy a fresh tropical cocktail served in a beautiful crystal parrot glass. Whether you are looking for a day-drinking cocktail in the city or the ideal poolside drink, Tipsy Parrot is a taste of an exotic paradise.

GLASSWARE: Crystal parrot glass

GARNISH: Wheat leaf, chocolate eggs

- 2 oz. | 60 ml tequila
- 1½ oz. | 45 ml passion fruit juice
- 1 oz. | 30 ml pineapple juice
- ½ oz. | 15 ml Liquore Strega
- ½ oz. | 15 ml simple syrup

1. Combine all of the ingredients in a cocktail shaker filled with ice.

2. Shake vigorously until chilled, then strain the cocktail into a crystal parrot glass.

3. Garnish with a wheat leaf and, as a side, chocolate eggs.

BLACKBERRY 75

LILŌU
CAMPOS ELÍSEOS 218 COL. POLANCO,
ALCALDÍA MIGUEL HIDALGO

Not only delicious, the Blackberry 75 is also very Instagram worthy, due to the dry ice reveal. Its relaxed yet elegant flavor is accompanied by vibrant colors.

GLASSWARE: Pitcher glass in a crystal sphere
covered with a crystal dome
GARNISH: Blackberries and lemon peels on
a skewer, dry ice and cloche

- 4 oz. | 120 ml Beefeater Blackberry Gin
- 1 oz. | 30 ml fresh lemon juice
- ½ oz. | 15 ml Juniper Syrup (see recipe)
- 8 oz. | 240 ml Champagne, to top
- Blackberry Jam (see recipe), to taste

1. Combine all of the ingredients, except for the Champagne, in a cocktail shaker with ice.
2. Shake vigorously until chilled.
3. Strain the cocktail into a pitcher glass and add the Champagne.
4. Garnish with blackberries and lemon peels on a skewer.
5. Place dry ice into the base of the crystal sphere, activate it with water, and cover the cocktail with a crystal dome to create a revealing effect when opened.

JUNIPER SYRUP: Place 15 juniper seeds and equal parts sugar and water—1 cup each—in a saucepan. Bring the mixture to a boil then lower the heat, stirring frequently, and reduce until the mixture becomes syrupy. Strain the syrup before using or storing.

BLACKBERRY JAM: Add 170 grams blackberries, ½ cup sugar, and the juice of 1 lemon to a small pot. Bring the mixture to a boil and stir until it thickens. Allow the jam to cool.

MARGARITA CADILLAC

RESTAURANTE NICOS
AVENIDA CUITLÁHUAC 3102, COL. CLAVERÍA,
ALCALDÍA AZCAPOTZALCO

Outside Nicos, one of Latin America's 50 Best Restaurants, there are two mandarin trees whose fruits are harvested every year to be used in the iconic Margarita Cadillac at the request of chef Gerardo Vázquez Lugo. This mandarin juice not only adds a special flavor to the cocktail, it also shares the essence and history of Nicos with their visitors.

GLASSWARE: Nick & Nora glass
GARNISH: Lime twist

- Citrus Salt (see recipe), for the rim
- 1½ oz. | 45 ml tequila
- 1 oz. | 30 ml Grand Marnier
- 1 oz. | 30 ml fresh lemon juice
- ½ oz. | 15 ml mandarin juice
- ½ oz. | 15 ml simple syrup

1. Wet the rim of the Nick & Nora and dip it into the citrus salt.

2. Add the remaining ingredients to a cocktail shaker filled with ice.

3. Shake vigorously until chilled and double-strain the cocktail into a Nick & Nora.

4. Garnish with a lime twist.

CITRUS SALT: Add equal parts lemon zest and orange zest for 3 parts fleur de sel.

MARGARITA YUZU KOSHO

SEÑORA TANAKA
AV. PDTE. MASARYK 169, COL. POLANCO,
ALCALDÍA MIGUEL HIDALGO

This cocktail gives a Japanese twist to the classic Margarita. The homemade yuzu salt combined with tequila creates a fresh flavor that will conquer all margarita lovers.

GLASSWARE: Rocks glass

GARNISH: Dehydrated lemon wheel

- 1½ oz. | 45 ml tequila
- 1 oz. | 30 ml cucumber pulp
- ½ oz. | 15 ml fresh lime juice
- ½ oz. | 15 ml agave nectar
- ¼ oz. | 7.5 ml yuzu kosho
- Yuzu Salt (see recipe), for the rim

1. Combine all of the ingredients in a cocktail shaker with ice and shake.

2. Wet the rim of a rocks glass then dip the glass in the Yuzu Salt.

3. Add an ice cube to the rocks glass.

4. Double-strain the cocktail into the glass.

5. Garnish with a dehydrated lemon wheel.

YUZU SALT: Add Maldon Sea Salt Flakes and yuzu juice to a container and mix thoroughly. Spread the mixture on wax paper and let it dehydrate.

NANCHE MARTINI

TICUCHI
FRANCISCO PETRARCA 254, COL. POLANCO,
ALCALDÍA MIGUEL HIDALGO

One of Ticuchi's first cocktails, of course, is an emblematic one. Highlighting mezcal, this cocktail is an example of a harmonious balance: profound yet ethereal where everything revolves around the garnish. Nanche, cured with salt, imparts an olive-like touch, perfuming the Martini. Looking for something to pair with this cocktail? Popcorn seasoned with worm salt is just heavenly! Use any manzanilla—fortified Andalusian white wine—as a substitute for the Navazos.

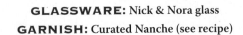

GLASSWARE: Nick & Nora glass

GARNISH: Curated Nanche (see recipe)

- 1¼ oz. | 37.5 ml Mezcal Espadín Koch
- ½ oz. | 15 ml Cocchi Americano
- ½ oz. | 15 ml Dolin Blanc Vermouth
- ¼ oz. | 7.5 ml Dolin Dry Vermouth
- ¼ oz. | 7.5 ml La Bota de Manzanilla Fino "Navazos"

1. Combine all of the ingredients in a cocktail shaker filled with ice.
2. Shake vigorously until chilled and strain the cocktail into a Nick & Nora.
3. Garnish with Curated Nanche.

CURATED NANCHE. For every kilogram (4 cups) of nanche add 1 liter (4 cups) water, 150 ml (5 oz.) white vinegar, and 50 grams (2¾ tablespoons) sea salt. Mix all of the ingredients and let it marinate for at least 5 days.

TOKOYA MARGARITA YUZU KOSHO

TOKOYA
CAMPOS ELÍSEOS 218, COL. POLANCO,
ALCALDÍA MIGUEL HIDALGO

Originally a barbershop at Hotel Presidente Intercontinental, Tokoya has transformed into a vibrant speakeasy where music, neon lights, mixology, and elevated Japanese gastronomy get a Mexican twist. This Margarita, created by Eimos D. Ayala, is likely one of the most delicious in Mexico City, combining tequila with Japanese ingredients.

* * *

GLASSWARE: Rocks glass

GARNISH: Roasted pineapple roll-up

* * *

- 1 tablespoon yuzu kosho
- Pinch habanero salt
- 2 oz. | 60 ml Don Julio 70 Tequila
- 2 oz. | 60 ml yuzu juice
- 1 oz. | 30 ml orange juice
- 1 oz. | 30 ml simple syrup

1. Wet the rim of a rocks glass with yuzu kosho and dip it into habanero salt.
2. Add the remaining ingredients to a cocktail shaker filled with ice.
3. Shake vigorously until chilled.
4. Double-strain the cocktail over ice into the rocks glass.
5. Garnish with roasted pineapple roll-up.

MICTLÁN

TRIVVU
CAMPOS ELÍSEOS 252, COL. POLANCO,
ALCALDÍA MIGUEL HIDALGO

The concept of Mictlán is rooted in the religious and mythological beliefs of the Mexicas and refers to the underworld, or the place of the dead. In Mexico, we celebrate the lives of and honor those who have departed every year on the Day of the Dead, at the end of October. Based on this concept, Christian Pérez created a cocktail for those who are in an extraordinary place as a tribute. In this elixir, ancestral flavors converge.

GLASSWARE: Rocks glass

GARNISH: Dehydrated chile de árbol, orange half-moon

- Worm Salt with Chile de Árbol (see recipe), for the rim
- 1½ oz. | 45 ml mezcal
- 1½ oz. | 45 ml Hibiscus Infusion (see recipe)
- 1 oz. | 30 ml simple syrup
- ½ oz. | 15 ml Ancho Reyes Original Chile Liqueur
- ½ oz. | 15 ml fresh lime juice

1. Wet the rim of the rocks glass and dip it into the Worm Salt with Chile de Árbol.
2. Add the remaining ingredients to a cocktail shaker filled with ice.
3. Shake vigorously until chilled and pour the cocktail into the rocks glass filled with ice.
4. Garnish with dehydrated chile de árbol and an orange half-moon.

HIBISCUS INFUSION: Make a loose-leaf hibiscus tea using cold water in stainless steel to not affect the pH of the hibiscus and preserve the essence and flavors of the flower.

WORM SALT WITH CHILE DE ÁRBOL: Add worm salt and dehydrated chile de árbol to a *metate* (a flat stone for grinding). Grind it in the artisanal way until a fine powder is obtained.

TANA

JULIO VERNE 84B COL. POLANCO
ALCALDÍA MIGUEL HIDALGO

Tana, which means "cave" in Italian, is a bar project of Raffaele Chinea (@rafachinea.foodrinks) that integrates the concept of the four elements: fire, water, air, and earth. This fusion is achieved through a balance of textures, sounds, and colors that culminates in an atmosphere reminiscent of a cavern. Just as caverns provide shelter, this bar offers a similar sense of refuge after a long workday.

With its large square table, Tana serves as a social bar where people can meet and connect while enjoying delicious cocktails and food. The table is an inverted pyramid designed by "Ra!"

Interior design plays an important role. Behind the bar, a large, illuminated copper plate, manufactured in Michoacán, frames the stage where the mixologist performs as a master of ceremonies.

VERDE MARÍA

TANA
JULIO VERNE 84B COL. POLANCO
ALCALDÍA MIGUEL HIDALGO

Raffaele Chinea's cocktail is prepared with a base of espadín mezcal, featuring an acidic touch of green tomato contrasted by lime. A reduction of agave nectar with serrano chile peppers is added for a spicy kick, and grasshopper salt—an Oaxacan specialty—enhances all the flavors.

GLASSWARE: Highball glass

GARNISH: Clarified tomato leaf

- 2 oz. | 60 ml mezcal espadín
- 1½ oz. | 45 ml green tomato juice
- ½ oz. | 15 ml fresh lime juice
- ½ oz. | 15 ml Agave Nectar and Serrano Reduction (see recipe)
- ½ oz. | 15 ml sparkling water
- 1 gram grasshopper salt (*sal de chapulín*)

1. Add a large, gourmet ice cube from a collins glass mold to a highball glass to chill the glass.
2. Combine all of the ingredients in a cocktail shaker filled with ice.
3. Throw the mixture four to five times to air the ingredients.
4. Strain the cocktail into the chilled highball and garnish with a clarified tomato leaf.

AGAVE NECTAR AND SERRANO REDUCTION:
In a small saucepan over low heat, combine 1 cup water and 1 cup agave nectar. Simmer, stirring, until the syrup reaches the consistency you prefer. Allow the syrup to cool then add 2 serrano chile peppers and steep for up to 24 hours. Strain before using.

NUBE

TANA
JULIO VERNE 84B COL. POLANCO,
ALCALDÍA MIGUEL HIDALGO

A fusion of Asian flavors, Nube ("cloud") is a vodka-based cocktail with a fiery kick of wasabi and the refreshing essence of shiso leaves that provide a zesty hint of citrus. Raffaele Chinea crafted this recipe to intensify all the flavors in the cocktail: the coriander oil acts a catalyzer of herbal notes, while the delicate rice cloud enveloping the wakame seaweed adds a salty contrast.

GLASSWARE: Coupe glass

GARNISH: Rice cloud with Wakame seaweed

- 2 oz. | 60 ml vodka
- 1 oz. | 30 ml fresh lime juice
- ⅔ oz. | 20 ml Wasabi Syrup with Shiso Leaves (see recipe)
- 1 piece of shiso leaf
- 3 drops coriander oil

1. Combine all the ingredients, except for the coriander oil, in a cocktail shaker filled with ice.
2. Shake vigorously until chilled, then double-strain the cocktail into a coupe.
3. Add the coriander oil.
4. Garnish with a rice cloud with Wakame seaweed.

WASABI SYRUP WITH SHISO LEAVES: In a pot, add 500 grams (2 cups) sugar and 500 ml (2 cups) water. Bring the mixture to a boil, allowing it to reduce until you achieve a syrup-like consistency, and then add wasabi, to taste and shiso leaves. Combine the syrup, let it cool, and reserve it.

SOL NACIENTE

BRASSI
VIRGILIO 8 COL. POLANCO, ALCALDÍA MIGUEL HIDALGO

Brassi stands as one of the timeless classics at Polanquito, where, with comfort food and drinks, they offer a cozy oasis for their guests. This fresh and aromatic cocktail was created by Giovanni Pérez for the Tanqueray Nº TEN competition. The Sol Naciente is a true metaphor that evokes the moment the sun goes down, inviting you to immerse yourself in a perfect sunset experience.

GLASSWARE: Balloon glass

GARNISH: Cardamom seeds, fresh basil leaves, grapefruit half-moon

---

- 2 oz. | 60 ml grapefruit juice
- 1 oz. | 30 ml Tanqueray Nº TEN
- 1 oz. | 30 ml Aperol
- ½ oz. | 15 ml fresh lime juice
- ⅓ oz. | 10 ml grenadine
- 2 grams cardamom seeds
- 5 grams fresh albahaca leaves
- 2 oz. | 60 ml sparkling water, to top

1. Combine all of the ingredients, except for the sparkling water, in a cocktail shaker filled with ice.
2. Shake vigorously until chilled.
3. Double-strain the cocktail into a balloon glass filled with ice and top with sparkling water.
4. Garnish with cardamom seeds, fresh basil leaves, and a half-moon of grapefruit.

LEMON CHEESECAKE

VILLA MASSA LIMONCELLO

Are you in the mood for dessert, but also for a refreshing cocktail? This Lemon Cheesecake is perfect. A symphony of creamy spices, zesty limoncello, and a hint of sweetness will make this drink an irresistible experience.

GLASSWARE: Martini glass

GARNISH: Lemon peel

- 1⅓ oz. | 40 ml Villa Massa Limoncello
- 1 oz. | 30 ml fresh lemon juice
- 1 oz. | 30 ml cream
- ⅔ oz. | 20 ml Licor 43
- ⅔ oz. | 20 ml simple syrup

1. Combine all of the ingredients in a cocktail shaker filled with ice.

2. Shake vigorously until chilled and strain the cocktail into a martini glass.

3. Garnish with a lemon peel.

GREEN SUIT

HERMITAGE
AV. PASEO DE LAS PALMAS 810, COL. LOMAS DE
CHAPULTEPEC, ALCALDÍA MIGUEL HIDALGO

Hermitage specializes in creating experiences around wine in an elegant French-inspired environment. This is the perfect place to learn to pair and try different grapes, especially in a fresh tropical cocktail, like this one from Laura Santander.

GLASSWARE: Rocks glass

GARNISH: Fresh rosemary sprig, slice of kiwi

- 2 oz. | 60 ml dry white wine
- 1 oz. | 30 ml Glenfiddich 12 Year Old Single Malt Scotch Whisky
- 1 oz. | 30 ml simple syrup
- ½ oz. | 15 ml fresh lime juice
- ½ piece kiwi, diced into cubes
- Basil leaves, as needed

1. Combine all of the ingredients in a cocktail shaker filled with ice.

2. Shake vigorously until chilled then strain the cocktail into a rocks glass filled with ice cubes.

3. Garnish with a sprig of fresh rosemary and a slice of kiwi.

VERDE VIDA

PISO CUATRO

AV. PASEO DE LAS PALMAS 530, COL. LOMAS DE
CHAPULTEPEC, ALCALDÍA MIGUEL HIDALGO

When a fine breeze is felt, and the rain starts to fall: that's when Tlaloc, the ancient Aztec god of the rain, reveals his presence. Crafted by Omar Pérez Carreño, this cocktail is green and full of life, fresh, and herbal.

GLASSWARE: Tlaloc tiki mug

GARNISH: Cucumber slices, blackberry

- 2 oz. | 60 ml Sweet and Sour Mix (see recipe)
- 1½ oz. | 45 ml mezcal
- ¼ oz. | 7.5 ml Green Chartreuse
- 4 cucumber slices
- Tonic water, to top

1. Combine all of the ingredients, except for the tonic water, in a cocktail shaker and muddle the cucumber.
2. Add ice cubes to the cocktail shaker and shake vigorously until chilled.
3. Strain the cocktail into the Tlaloc tiki mug filled with ice cubes and top with tonic water.
4. Garnish with cucumber slices and a blackberry.

SWEET AND SOUR MIX: Use equal parts lime juice and simple syrup. Mix it and reserve it.

LESLIE JAIME, MISS COCTEL

It all began with Ginstone, a collaborative project between Leslie Jaime (@misscoctel) and her brother, who were inspired to create something transcendent, distinct, and unique and offer an atypical gin in a highly competitive market. For Leslie, Ginstone was the driver to share her passion for the mixology world, and so it was that Miss Coctel emerged as a platform where Leslie shares her insights and experiences of bar culture.

What makes your brand unique?

As of today, Ginstone is the most-awarded Mexican gin in the world, winning a silver medal at the San Francisco World Spirit Competition, Highscorer in the Gin Guide Awards in London, and a bronze at the New Orleans Spirit Competition by Tales of the Cocktail. Now there are two brands—Ginstone and Galénico—both compound gins inspired by the Dutch style. Ginstone has a complex profile with notes of fennel, citrus, and peppers, while Galénico is an overproof with a much more traditional profile featuring intense notes of juniper, almonds, toffee, caramel, orange, and cherry.

What led you to explore The World's 50 Best Bars and share your experience on social media?

I have always been passionate about traveling. Initially, with Miss Coctel, my mission was to travel to the The World's 50 Best Bars, but the pandemic arrived, forcing me to rethink the project. Now, after three years, I am in the process of reactivating Around the World in 50 Bars, where we explore the best bars globally and share my experiences on YouTube for an audience that includes enthusiasts and industry professionals who want to see what is happening in their fields in other countries.

Which are the must-visit bars for cocktail enthusiasts in Mexico City?

Without a doubt, the number one is Handshake Speakeasy. Their level of mixology is the highest in the country in terms of techniques, textures, processes, and the impressive production lab. The overall experience at the bar is unique and not to be missed. Limantour is another bar to visit as a pioneer in mixology in Mexico, drawing the world's attention to Mexico from its inception. The third is Casa Prunes, a bar in an Art Nouveau–style house offering incredible gastronomy along with one of the warmest hospitalities in the city.

What makes a bar stand out as one of the best in the world?

It is definitely a combination of many factors, with the ultimate goal being to create a memorable experience for guests. To achieve this, the three points I would highlight as crucial are 1) hospitality—feeling welcomed, well served, and comfortable with your host is fundamental; 2) mixology—there cannot be a good bar without good cocktails; and finally, 3) the design and ambience of the bar—it's important to feel so comfortable that I could spend hours without moving, with appropriate lighting and music, comfortable furniture, and good planning in the bar layout to create a cohesive and memorable experience.

What is your vision of the future of mixology in Mexico?

The future of mixology in Mexico is starting to be built now, with a much better communicated and amplified culture toward consumers and a more competitive industry focused on standing out globally. Currently, brands, bartenders, entrepreneurs, and all links in the chain together have propelled a wave of global exposure. Even now, bars outside of Mexico City are beginning to make waves worldwide, substantially contributing to the exposure of our mixology scene and, above all, raising the standards of bars in every corner of the country.

FIGLET

GINSTONE

A perfectly balanced cocktail where the aromatic gin, the rich sweetness of fig cordial, and the herbal complexity of vermouth bianco turn into a smooth and harmonious blend.

GLASSWARE: Nick & Nora glass

- **1½ oz. | 45 ml Ginstone**
- **1⅓ oz. | 40 ml Fig Cordial (see recipe)**
- **⅓ oz. | 10 ml vermouth bianco**
- **Pink peppercorn, to perfume**

1. Chill a Nick & Nora glass. Add all of the ingredients to a mixing glass filled with ice cubes.
2. Stir until chilled.
3. Strain the cocktail into the chilled Nick & Nora.
4. Perfume the drink with pink peppercorn.

FIG CORDIAL: Sous vide 1 liter water, 300 grams sugar, 100 grams fig leaves, and 60 grams citric acid at 122°F (50°C) for 2 hours.

IVÁN SALDAÑA, CASA LUMBRE

What happens when your passion for biology, scientific curiosity, and research of resilient plants such as agave intersects with the art of distillation? Master distiller Iván Saldaña co-founded Casa Lumbre along with Moisés Guindi and Daniel Schneeweiss. Being a specialist in raw materials, Iván has always seen himself as a storyteller within a company that's capable of crafting a liquid experience that captures the essence of Mexico.

Considered one of the top 100 most creative Mexicans according to *Forbes Mexico*, Iván developed his Mezcal Montelobos and later crafted the iconic spicy cocktail ingredient Ancho Reyes, a handmade liqueur made from ancho chile peppers and chile poblanos in Puebla, Mexico. As of today, Casa Lumbre has created fifteen solid and disruptive brands such as Nixta Licor de Elote, a corn liqueur made from tender cacahuazintle maize; Abasolo, an ancestral corn whiskey; Alma Finca, an orange liqueur that pays tribute to Yucatan's flowers and citrus; and Gin Las Californias, which involved expeditions to collect plants in Upper and Lower (Alta and Baja) California.

Their most recent project is Almave, a nonalcoholic blue agave spirit from Los Altos de Jalisco, produced in partnership with the seven-time Formula 1 world champion Lewis Hamilton.

What's the importance of preserving cultural, biological, and sensory heritage in the production of Mexican spirits?

Mexico is one of the richest countries with more history in flavor and biological diversity . . . We understand that most traditional products that are converted into alcohol in Mexico have a heritage, a history that is in the hands of generations of families, mezcal and tequila masters. They captured a legacy that is ours and ours nationally, which is flavor. Therefore, historical taste is very important; it is culturally constructed through families.

Spirits are made from raw materials which contain sugar transformed into alcohol that impart flavor. So, not preserving what is authentic is essentially to create something without a soul. Casa Lumbre is a company founded in the possibility of rescuing raw materials, techniques, traditional processes in the production of alcoholic beverages, and then present them dignified, transformed, reinterpreted so that everyone else can know them and hopefully enjoy them too.

What makes your spirits unique? What's the process of conceptualizing a new product?

We have a highly intuitive creative process, with Moisés, my partner, possessing a keen sense for business opportunities. He serves as a constant antenna, presenting challenges or pointing out potential business opportunities. This has been a great catalyst for me to begin the product development process in the laboratory. On the other hand, Daniel comes in at a later stage, and his leadership lies in creating the look and feel and packaging of the product. This can only be done coherently once the story and the liquid have been invented. It must reflect the essence of the product, and the product is what's inside.

So, within Casa Lumbre, we have, I would say, two processes: a conceptual and executional. One involving the creation of authentic brands, mantras, very specific bullet points. For example, the relationship with the place of origin, the heritage that involves cultural elements of the product's origin and raw materials. There is a phase of research; we recently released a Yucatán orange liqueur called Alma Finca. Its development involved trips, talking to people, gathering raw materials, cutting leaves, flowers, taking them to the laboratory, seeing what aromas they give, and conducting experiments. Then we start telling a story about a town, what it used to do, what it did before, how citrus came to Yucatán, why it's important. This exploration allows us to present a consistent and coherent brand. We also work with cooperatives to supply all our raw materials, and in the laboratory, we do experiments. Afterwards, a marketing team is analyzing if this is viable, how it will be received, who it is important for, who our competitors are. It's an extensive team effort.

In the end, we come up with a proposal that we launch into the market, and the most challenging part is proving that the product goes from zero to a certain number of units or gains recognition. That's when we believe that what we produce matters. When someone dares to open their wallet and pay for an experience in the store or at the bar by purchasing a Casa Lumbre spirit, that's when we truly begin. Four people started, and today we are almost 500.

Are you working on some other projects?

We are making investments to improve and develop much more sustainable agronomic projects. In Puebla, we have a project to convert areas that were used for sugarcane cultivation, which are completely eroded, into maguey cultivation. We are also making technological innovations, understanding processes better. For example, how to bake in an oven using less firewood. How to cultivate a plant that has never been planted, like the dasylirion or sotol, establishing plantations.

In agriculture and processes, we are working a lot. Also, innovative products like nonalcoholic beverages, offering the world drinks that represent incredible raw materials like agave and are perfect for times for drinking that, until now, alcohol has dominated. We will continue to try to make better spirits with a smaller environmental impact and a broader cultural, biological, and sensory richness.

Tell us more about Anatomía del Mezcal?

I completed a PhD that took four and a half years and, before entering the spirits industry, my focus was on understanding the natural history of agave from the perspective of the evolutionary solutions I had to create. Then, I spent six years learning to distill. These two experiences led me to realize that I had to express this in a very simple way, in a tiny booklet I wrote ten years ago. It has never been sold; it was never intended to be pretentious; I am committed to that cultural aspect. Although I have been very busy creating brands, I hope to continue contributing in my role as an educator, providing access to that information.

ALMA FINCA WHITE LADY

CASA LUMBRE

Simplicity, elegance, and sophistication best describe the classic White Lady cocktail, which was created in the early twentieth century. True to its name, this version has a pale, almost ethereal appearance that reflects Yucatan's citrusy essence with notes of fresh sweet and bitter oranges, Persian limes, blossoms, and spices.

GLASSWARE: Coupe glass

- 2 oz. | 60 ml Gin de Las Californias Nativo
- ½ oz. | 15 ml Alma Finca Orange Liqueur
- ½ oz. | 15 ml fresh lime juice
- 1 egg white

1. Chill a coupe glass. Combine all of the ingredients in a cocktail shaker filled with ice.
2. Shake vigorously until chilled.
3. Strain the cocktail into the chilled coupe.

ATACAMA SUNSET

CASA LUMBRE

Atacama, a Chilean region famed for having the driest desert on earth, is probably one of the most breathtaking places to watch the sun set and transition into a perfect starry night. Of course, it's impossible to talk about Chile without mentioning pisco, its national spirit. Blended with mezcal, it creates a unique fusion of smoked and citrus flavors unlike any other.

GLASSWARE: Highball glass

GARNISH: Lemongrass

- 1 oz. | 30 ml Pisco Telum
- 1 oz. | 30 ml agave nectar
- 1 oz. | 30 ml mango juice
- ¾ oz. | 22.5 ml Mezcal Amarás Cupreata Joven
- ½ oz. | 15 ml Passion Fruit Pulp (see recipe on page 141)
- ½ oz. | 15 ml fresh lemon juice

1. Combine all of the ingredients in a cocktail shaker filled with ice.

2. Shake vigorously until chilled.

3. Strain the cocktail into a highball filled with one collins ice cube.

4. Garnish with lemongrass.

LA ROMA

MEZCALITA DE PIÑA	COATL
TATEMADA	THE REAL
MARTÍNEZ	SLIM SHADY
NO FIG-URATIVO	TEJUINO
TROPICAL CYCLONE	TONIC 77
BABERO SBAGLIATO	GALLITO
BROKA	MARTINI DE
BOCANADA	HOJA SANTA
SANTO APERITIVO	PALOMA BLANCA
WHITE CALYPSO	WILSON MAI TAI
THE LAST RUSSIAN	GIMLET
IRREGULAR HIGHBALL	OROPEL
CARAJILLO MADRE	OZAIN
LUNA AZUL	TÉ DE CHARLIE
CAMP OF RUM	MILLE
MARTÍNEZ SPRITZ	LAWER
PEAR-DICIÓN	2244

La Roma is a neighborhood of happy memories and people, incredible gastronomical projects, plenty of cheerful dogs, and . . . pet pigs. Yep, that's how captivating this bohemian, *cough, cough* hipster/digital nomad neighborhood is. Exploring La Roma is an enchanting experience that triggers your curiosity to discover new coffee shops, bakeries, vintage boutiques, bookstores, and art galleries at every turn. From hidden gems like Tlecan, which will make you feel proud of being Mexican or happy to be visiting Mexico, to outstanding signature cocktails in almost every bar, and incredibly nice rooftops boasting the perfect soundtrack, La Roma is pure magic.

MEZCALITA DE PIÑA TATEMADA

3 TONALÁ
TONALÁ 171 COL. ROMA NORTE, ALCALDÍA CUAUHTÉMOC

This cocktail highlights the fertile chinampas of Xochimilco. Created by Luis Vaquero, this drink is designed to be enjoyed year-round, featuring readily available ingredients that capture the essence of Mexican culture. If you are serving among people with peanut allergies, skip the peanut salt.

* * *

GLASSWARE: Rocks glass

GARNISH: Dehydrated pineapple slice

* * *

- **Peanut Salt (see recipe), for the rim**
- **1½ oz. | 45 ml mezcal espadín joven**
- **1½ oz. | 45 ml Nixta Licor de Elote**
- **1½ oz. | 45 ml grapefruit juice**
- **1 oz. | 30 ml Roasted Pineapple & Spices Syrup (see recipe)**

1. Wet the rim of a rocks glass and dip it into the Peanut Salt.

2. Combine all of the ingredients in a cocktail shaker filled with ice.

3. Shake vigorously until chilled.

4. Strain the cocktail into the rocks glass.

5. Garnish with a dehydrated pineapple slice.

PEANUT SALT: Roast 1 cup unsalted peanuts until golden brown, then cool them. Crush the cooled peanuts finely and mix them with ¼ cup sea salt. Store the resulting peanut salt in a salt shaker.

ROASTED PINEAPPLE & SPICES SYRUP: Grill 600 grams pineapple on a cast iron griddle. Once the pineapple has cooled, put it in the blender with 500 ml (2 cups) water and 300 grams (1½ cups) white sugar and blend. After blending, strain the mixture to remove the excess fibers, then simmer it in a saucepan for 10 minutes with 7 grams cinnamon sticks, 3 grams (1 teaspoon) pink peppercorns, 1 gram cloves, and 1 gram star anise. Let the mixture cool, then bottle it, label it, and store it in the refrigerator before use.

MARTÍNEZ

686 BAR
TONALÁ 133, 2DO PISO, COL. ROMA NORTE,
ALCALDÍA CUAUHTÉMOC

This cocktail embodies the art of reimagining a classic cocktail recipe with the distinctively native spirit from Chihuahua: sotol.

GLASSWARE: Nick & Nora glass

- **1½ oz. | 45 ml Dolin Rouge Vermouth**
- **1 oz. | 30 ml Los Magos Sotol Blanco**
- **½ oz. | 15 ml pacharán**
- **Dash citric bitters**

1. Chill a Nick & Nora glass. Combine all of the ingredients in a mixing glass filled with ice.

2. Stir until chilled, or around 45 seconds.

3. Strain the cocktail into the chilled Nick & Nora.

NO FIG-URATIVO

1985 ANTIFINE
ORIZABA 76 COL. ROMA NORTE,
ALCALDÍA CUAUHTÉMOC

The No Fig-Urativo is a cocktail born from a fusion of aromas, memories, and the boundless creativity of visionary bartender Miguel Rocha. This mesmerizing elixir engages your senses, and with its name, Rocha invites you to interpret what comes to your mind with each sip you take.

GLASSWARE: Coupe glass

GARNISH: Rice wafer with edible non-figurative art

- 1½ oz. | 45 ml white vermouth
- ½ oz. | 15 ml bourbon
- ½ oz. | 15 ml aged rum
- ½ oz. | 15 ml Damiana Liqueur
- ½ oz. | 15 ml Lemon Sherbet Cordial (see recipe)
- Fig Leaf Oil (see recipe), to taste

1. Combine all of the ingredients, except for the oil, in a mixing glass filled with ice.
2. Stir until chilled and all ingredients are combined.
3. Strain the cocktail into a coupe.
4. Add some drops of Fig Leaf Oil over the top and garnish with a rice wafer with edible non-figurative art.

LEMON SHERBET CORDIAL: Add 30 grams (2 tablespoons) lemon zest, 180 grams (6 oz.) sugar, 750 ml (3 cups) water, 15 grams (1 tablespoon) malic acid, and 20 grams (1¼ tablespoons) citric acid to a vacuum bag. Once the bag is sealed, keep it in a sous vide at 140°F (60°C) for 25 minutes. After this time, perform a thermal shock and filter the cordial.

FIG LEAF OIL: Add canola oil and fig leaves without stems to a Thermomix (or use a blender), and process at 140°F (60°C) for 10 minutes.

TROPICAL CYCLONE

ALOFAH TIKI BAR
COAHUILA 49 COL. ROMA NORTE,
ALCALDÍA CUAUHTÉMOC

Tangaroa, the inspiration for this tiki mug, is the offspring of gods Rangi and Papa who ruled over the seas, fish, and reptiles, conjuring waves that devoured entire lands. This cocktail combines tropical flavors, aged Caribbean rum, a hint of sweet and sour tamarind from Michoacán, and the richness of vanilla from Veracruz. It's a secret off-menu cocktail, known only to the inner circle—like you!—which can be ordered with the words, "It's said that a cyclone passed through here."

GLASSWARE: Tiki mug of Tangaroa

GARNISH: Mint sprig, orange wedge, Luxardo cherry

- 2 oz. | 60 ml aged rum
- 1½ oz. | 45 ml orange juice
- ¾ oz. | 22.5 ml tamarind pulp
- ¾ oz. | 22.5 ml melon liqueur
- ½ oz. | 15 ml fresh lemon juice
- Barspoon vanilla extract

1. Combine all of the ingredients in a cocktail shaker filled with crushed ice.
2. Shake vigorously until chilled.
3. Strain the cocktail into the tiki mug filled with crushed ice.
4. Garnish with a fresh mint sprig, an orange wedge, and a Luxardo cherry.

BABERO SBAGLIATO

BABERO

DURANGO 219 COL. ROMA NORTE,
ALCALDÍA CUAUHTÉMOC

Brutalism, an architectural style derived from the French term *béton brut*, meaning "raw concrete," is defined by its use of organic materials such as concrete complemented by geometric designs, an example of which is the remarkable Babero. This design concept, where simplicity prevails as "less is more," has extended into its Brutalist cocktails that accentuate the pure essences of their flavors. The Babero Sbagliato, created by Julio César Delgado, exemplifies this philosophy by embracing the elegance of simplicity, allowing each ingredient to shine in its truest form.

GLASSWARE: Rocks glass

GARNISH: Grapefruit Coin (see recipe)

- 2 oz. | 60 ml prosecco
- 1 oz. | 30 ml Cocchi Rosa
- 1 oz. | 30 ml Cocchi Americano
- 2 drops spiced bitters
- Grapefruit peel, to aromatize

1. Combine all of the ingredients, except for the grapefruit peel, in a mixing glass filled with ice.
2. Stir until chilled.
3. Strain the cocktail into a rocks glass and aromatize it with a grapefruit peel.
4. Garnish with a grapefruit coin.

GRAPEFRUIT COIN: Use a zester to create a long strip of grapefruit peel. Then, carefully cut the strip into a circular or coin-like shape.

BROKA

BROKA BISTROT
ZACATECAS 126, COL. ROMA NORTE,
ALCALDÍA CUAUHTÉMOC

Broka: a signature cocktail crafted in Broka Bistrot's enchanting patio, nestled in one of Mexico City's most historic and beautiful neighborhoods. This cocktail is a creation born from a collaborative effort, celebrated by many, with no ownership except what each one brings to the glass.

GLASSWARE: Rocks glass

GARNISH: Dehydrated fruit

- **Hibiscus Salt (see recipe), for the rim**
- **1 oz. | 30 ml mezcal**
- **1 oz. | 30 ml Ancho Reyes Original Chile Liqueur**
- **1 oz. | 30 ml aquafaba**
- **1 oz. | 30 ml hibiscus cordial**
- **1 oz. | 30 ml fresh lemon juice**
- **1 oz. | 30 ml simple syrup**

1. Wet the rim of a rocks glass and dip it into the Hibiscus Salt.

2. Combine all of the ingredients in a cocktail shaker filled with ice.

3. Shake vigorously until chilled then strain the cocktail over ice cubes into the rocks glass.

4. Garnish with dehydrated fruit.

HIBISCUS SALT: In a mortar and pestle bowl, combine sea salt and dehydrated hibiscus flowers in a ratio of 90 percent salt, 10 percent flowers. Grind the ingredients.

BOCANADA

CAFÉ DE NADIE
CHIHUAHUA 135 COL. ROMA NORTE,
ALCALDÍA CUAUHTÉMOC

This cocktail's name pays tribute to one of the most iconic Latin rock albums by Gustavo Cerati, and simultaneously, this drink is like a *bocanada*, or "breath of fresh air." It's incredibly refreshing and easy to sip, yet rich and complex in flavors, with a generous kick of alcohol. Furthermore, it's a tribute to the network of local farmers Café de Nadie collaborates with, particularly the farmers of Arca Tierra who tend to the chinampas in Xochimilco. The star ingredient is kale, sourced from within Mexico City.

GLASSWARE: Rocks glass

GARNISH: Lime wedge, sprig of fresh scarlet kale

- 1½ oz. | 45 ml Kale Fat Washed–Raicilla (see recipe)
- ¾ oz. | 22.5 ml fino sherry
- Tonic water, to top

1. Combine all of the ingredients, except for the tonic water, in a mixing glass filled with ice.
2. Stir until chilled then strain the cocktail over ice cubes into a rocks glass.
3. Top with tonic water and garnish with a lime wedge and a sprig of fresh scarlet kale.

KALE FAT WASHED–RAICILLA: Infuse together 10 grams scarlet kale, 70 grams fresh avocado leaves, 200 ml (6¾ oz.) avocado oil, and 1 (750 ml) bottle of Raicilla La Venenosa. Place the mixture in a ziplock bag and heat at 158°F (70°C) for 2 hours. Refrigerate overnight. Strain and bottle.

SANTO APERITIVO

EM
TONALÁ 133, COL. ROMA NORTE,
ALCALDÍA CUAUHTÉMOC

Em uses a variety of techniques to reshape locally sourced ingredients with rich traditions into unique and unconventional creations. In this cocktail, the infusion of sacred leaf syrup, also known as hoja santa, contributes to create a multifaceted flavor profile.

GLASSWARE: Rocks glass

GARNISH: Lemon slice

- 1½ oz. | 45 ml Hoja Santa Syrup (see recipe)
- 1 oz. | 30 ml Carpano Dry
- ½ oz. | 15 ml pacharán
- 1 oz. | 30 ml Cinzano Rosso

1. Build the cocktail in a rocks glass containing ice cubes, following the order of ingredients as listed.

2. Stir to combine.

3. Garnish with a lemon slice.

HOJA SANTA SYRUP: Place hoja santa leaves and equal parts sugar and water in a saucepan. Bring the mixture to a boil, allowing it to reduce until you achieve a syrup-like consistency. Let it cool, then strain the syrup and reserve it.

WHITE CALYPSO

GYPSY
CÓRDOBA 49, COL. ROMA NORTE,
ALCALDÍA CUAUHTÉMOC

This cocktail is based on taste rather than techniques, flavor over power, simple but not easy; it's where Parisian elegance fuses with Australian influences into a Mexican cocktail designed by Nicolás Cruz.

✳

GLASSWARE: Cider glass
GARNISH: Grapefruit twist

- ¾ oz. | 22.5 ml Amargo Mexicano Milk Punch (see recipe)
- ½ oz. | 15 ml Pineapple Syrup (see recipe)
- ½ oz. | 15 ml fresh lime juice
- ½ oz. | 15 ml coconut water
- ¼ oz. | 7.5 ml Carpano Classico

1. Combine all of the ingredients in a mixing glass filled with ice.

2. Stir until chilled then strain the cocktail over a premium ice cube into a cider glass.

3. Garnish with a grapefruit twist.

AMARGO MEXICANO MILK PUNCH: Using Amargo-Vallet Cortezas de Angostura Liqueur as your base spirit, create a milk punch in a glass jar with warm milk, as needed, and an acidic ingredient such as citric acid or lemon juice, to taste. (You can also play around with spices in the recipe.) The milk will curdle and solidify out of the mixture and drop to the bottom of the jar. Over a 24-hour period, periodically strain the punch through a cheesecloth to clarify until the punch runs clear.

PINEAPPLE SYRUP: Place pineapple, to taste, and equal parts sugar and water in a saucepan. Bring the mixture to a boil, allowing it to reduce until you achieve a syrup-like consistency. Let it cool, then strain the syrup.

THE LAST RUSSIAN

JARDÍN CHAPULTEPEC
AV. CHAPULTEPEC 398 COL. ROMA NORTE,
ALCALDÍA CUAUHTÉMOC

In the middle of the concrete jungle that is Mexico City, an open garden emerges like an oasis. This is the place where Erik Israel González has concocted a refreshing cocktail that proves that simplicity is not the same as plain. Inspired by the classic Last Word, Erik's idea was to create a contrast between a strong alcohol kick and ice cream. This one is best served on a sunny day on the terrace.

GLASSWARE: Julep cup

GARNISH: 2 to 3 scoops lemon ice cream in a cucumber wrap

- 1 oz. | 30 ml Stoli Cucumber Vodka
- ¾ oz. | 22.5 ml fresh lime juice
- ½ oz. | 15 ml maraschino liqueur
- ½ oz. | 15 ml Ancho Reyes Verde Chile Liqueur
- ⅓ oz. | 10 ml Green Chartreuse

1. Combine all of the ingredients in a cocktail shaker filled with ice.
2. Shake vigorously until chilled.
3. Double-strain the cocktail into a julep cup or stainless-steel glass.
4. Add crushed ice and garnish with lemon ice-cream scoops in a cucumber wrap.

IRREGULAR HIGHBALL

LADINA BAR
COLIMA 333 COL. ROMA NORTE,
ALCALDÍA CUAUHTÉMOC

There's a special challenge in creating balance between ingredients that, in theory, don't pair well together, while allowing minimalism and sophistication to prevail. Created by Fabián Velázquez, philosophy graduate by education, bartender by vocation, this cocktail accepts the challenge.

GLASSWARE: Highball glass

GARNISH: Pickles on a skewer; perfume of pickle brine

- 1½ oz. | 45 ml sparkling wine
- 1½ oz. | 45 ml sparking water
- 1⅓ oz. | 40 ml Giffard Rhubarbe Liqueur
- 1⅓ oz. | 40 ml Mezcal Los Siete Misterios Doba-Yej
- ¼ oz. | 7.5 ml Smooth Acid Cordial (see recipe)

1. Following the order of the ingredients as listed, build the cocktail in a highball glass filled with ice cubes.

2. Stir softly until chilled and combined.

3. Garnish with pickles on a skewer and the perfume of pickle brine.

SMOOTH ACID CORDIAL: Add 500 ml (2 cups) water, 250 grams (1 cup) sugar, 20 grams (1¼ tablespoons) malic acid, and 20 grams (1¼ tablespoons) tartaric acid to a blender and mix. Refrigerate the cordial until ready to use.

CARAJILLO MADRE

MADRE CAFÉ
CDA. ORIZABA 131, COL. ROMA NORTE,
ALCALDÍA CUAUHTÉMOC

This cocktail blends the smoothness of horchata liqueur with the freshness of vodka. The blue spirulina together with garden flowers contributes to this drink being one of the favorite carajillos among customers at Madre Café.

GLASSWARE: Snifter glass

GARNISH: Cardamom powder, garden flower

- 2 oz. | 60 ml Licor 43 Horchata
- 2 oz. | 60 ml coconut milk
- 1 oz. | 30 ml Grey Goose Vodka
- 1 oz. | 30 ml evaporated milk
- 1 gram blue spirulina

1. Combine all of the ingredients in a cocktail shaker filled with ice.
2. Shake vigorously until chilled, or for 10 seconds.
3. Strain the cocktail into a snifter and garnish with cardamom and a garden flower.

LUNA AZUL

MADRE ROOF
CDA. ORIZABA 131, COL. ROMA NORTE,
ALCALDÍA CUAUHTÉMOC

This masterpiece harmoniously combines the botanical flavors of the gin and the freshness of citrus notes with a touch of mystery from the absinthe. Here, the night and the fairies will create a new taste that is hard to beat, tempting you to book a flight to Mexico City and visit just for Madre Roof's cocktails.

GLASSWARE: Spherical double-bottomed glass

GARNISH: Leaf skeleton or garden flower

- 1½ oz. | 45 ml Hendrix Orbium Gin
- ¾ oz. | 22.5 ml Hpnotiq
- ¾ oz. | 22.5 ml simple syrup
- ½ oz. | 15 ml absinthe
- ½ oz. | 15 ml fresh lime juice
- ⅓ oz. | 10 ml blue curaçao

1. Combine all of the ingredients in a mixing glass and stir for 25 seconds without ice, and then add 5 ice cubes and stir until chilled, or for 22 seconds.
2. Strain the cocktail into a spherical double-bottomed glass.
3. Garnish with a leaf skeleton or garden flower.

CAMP OF RUM

TERRAZA TONALÁ
TONALÁ 171, COL. ROMA NORTE,
ALCALDÍA CUAUHTÉMOC

A fresh and light cocktail ideal for relaxation or as an aperitif, Camp of Rum was crafted by Samantha Casco Santana. This venue is known for its selection of happy, chill, and fresh cocktails perfect for after-office hours. If you're adventurous, you can choose to make your own toasted marshmallow syrup.

GLASSWARE: Highball glass
GARNISH: Toasted marshmallow, bamboo skewer

- 1½ oz. | 45 ml Ron Matusalem Gran Reserva 15 Años
- 1½ oz. | 45 ml fresh pineapple juice
- ½ oz. | 15 ml Mancino Vermouth Rosso Amaranto
- ½ oz. | 15 ml fresh lime juice
- ½ oz. | 15 ml Monin Toasted Marshmallow Syrup
- Lavender tincture, to taste

1. Combine all of the ingredients in a cocktail shaker filled with ice.
2. Shake vigorously until chilled and dirty-pour (don't strain) the cocktail into a highball.
3. Add crushed ice to top and garnish with a toasted marshmallow and bamboo skewer

MARTÍNEZ SPRITZ

MARTÍNEZ
PUEBLA 90 COL. ROMA NORTE,
ALCALDÍA CUAUHTÉMOC

Authentic, relaxed, and friendly—that's the atmosphere where this cocktail was crafted in the heart of Mexico City. The result of this recipe is a tropical and sparkling mix.

GLASSWARE: Wineglass
GARNISH: Pollen

- 1½ oz. | 45 ml Banyan white wine
- 1 oz. | 30 ml passion fruit juice
- 1 oz. | 30 ml Cinzano Rosso
- ½ oz. | 15 ml simple syrup
- Sparkling wine, to top

1. Build the cocktail in a wineglass containing ice cubes and stir to combine.
2. Top with sparkling wine and garnish with pollen.

PEAR-DICIÓN

MEROMA
COLIMA 150, COL. ROMA NORTE,
ALCALDÍA CUAUHTÉMOC

Rodo Sánchez has always loved art and everything it entails—creativity, experimentation, self-expression, and the unique ability to share it—and the same concepts apply when creating new cocktails.

GLASSWARE: Coupe glass

GARNISH: Pear slice

- Absinthe, to rinse
- 1½ oz. | 45 ml tequila blanco
- 1 oz. | 30 ml Prosecco & Eucalyptus Syrup (see recipe)
- ½ oz. | 15 ml fresh lime juice
- ¼ butter pear

1. Rinse the inside of the coupe with absinthe, pour out the excess, and reduce the alcoholic graduation by flaming it.

2. Add the remaining ingredients to a cocktail shaker and muddle the pear.

3. Add ice cubes and shake vigorously until chilled.

4. Double-strain the cocktail into the coupe and garnish with a pear slice.

PROSECCO & EUCALYPTUS SYRUP: Place 30 to 40 eucalyptus leaves, 1 gram (½ teaspoon) ground cardamom, 1 gram (½ teaspoon) ground pink pepper, 350 grams (1½ cups) refined sugar, 250 ml (1 cup) water, and 1 (750 ml) bottle of prosecco brut in a saucepan. Bring it to a boil, reduce until syrupy. Strain and set aside.

COATL

MIGRANTE
CHIAPAS 196, COL. ROMA NORTE,
ALCALDÍA CUAUHTÉMOC

In the case of this cocktail, *el amor entra por los ojos*—"love enters through the eyes." The garnishes are simple but elegant, a visual pleasure that complements the exquisite flavors.

GLASSWARE: Vintage champagne glass

GARNISH: Volcanic stone, purple quelite

- 1½ oz. | 45 ml Beet Potion (see recipe)
- 1 oz. | 30 ml Tequila Tres Generaciones Plata
- ½ oz. | 15 ml fresh lime juice

1. Combine all of the ingredients in a mixing glass with ice.
2. Stir until chilled, or for 20 seconds.
3. Add a volcanic stone into a vintage champagne glass and strain the cocktail over the stone.
4. Garnish with a purple quelite placed over the volcanic stone.

BEET POTION: Blend 500 grams (1 pound) beets with 100 ml (3⅓ oz.) water. Place the mixture in a vacuum-sealed bag and add 360 ml (1½ cups) chili liqueur, 240 ml (1 cup) amaretto liqueur, and 300 grams (1½ cups) sugar. Seal the vacuum bag and let it rest for 3 hours. Strain and refrigerate it.

THE REAL SLIM SHADY

MUSAK
TONALÁ 171 COL. ROMA NORTE,
ALCALDÍA CUAUHTÉMOC

This bar was designed to be a hi-fi listening bar, featuring the best sounds in Mexico City. The cocktails are inspired by musicians, their songs, and their stories. Eminem's "The Real Slim Shady" was the muse for José Carlos del Valle Sánchez to craft an irreverent cocktail, aiming to inspire others to remain unique, no matter how strangely simple the mix may be.

* * *

GLASSWARE: Highball glass

GARNISH: Dehydrated grapefruit slice, lime peel, orange peel

- 1½ oz. | 45 ml mezcal espadín joven
- ⅓ oz. | 10 ml Ancho Reyes Verde Chile Poblano Liqueur
- 5 drops Citrus & Hibiscus Ink (see recipe)
- 3 drops Serrano Chile Ink (see recipe)
- 4 oz. | 120 ml tonic water, to top

1. Build the cocktail in a highball containing ice cubes, in the order listed.
2. Stir gently to combine.
3. Garnish with a dehydrated grapefruit slice, lime peel, and orange peel.

CITRUS & HIBISCUS INK: Add Valenciana orange peels, lime peels, 1 clove head, a tip of star anise, and 3 fresh hibiscus flowers in 180 ml (6 oz.) neutral alcohol (vodka, for example), let it sit for no less than 48 hours.

SERRANO CHILE INK: Add 150 grams (1¼ cups) deveined and seedless serrano chiles in 180 ml (6 oz.) neutral alcohol, and let it sit for no less than 48 hours.

TEJUINO

MUX RESTAURANTE
JALAPA 189, COL. ROMA NORTE,
ALCALDÍA CUAUHTÉMOC

Mexico has a vast culture where some traditions and beliefs are still not fully known. At places like Mux Restaurante, culinary traditions are brought to life. Beverages such as the Tejuino will give you a taste of cultural history.

GLASSWARE: Rocks glass

GARNISH: Lime slice

- Salt, for the rim
- 4 oz. | 120 ml Tejuino (see recipe)
- 1½ oz. | 45 ml Cascahuín Tequila Blanco
- 1 oz. | 30 ml fresh lime juice

1. Wet the rim of a rocks glass and dip it into the salt.

2. Combine all of the ingredients in a cocktail shaker filled with ice and shake vigorously until chilled.

3. Strain the cocktail into the rocks glass filled with three ice cubes.

4. Garnish with a lime slice.

TEJUINO: Add 400 grams (2½ cups) masa (corn dough) and 1 liter (4 cups) water into a saucepan. Dissolve the mixture completely, avoiding lumps. Bring it to a boil, adding cinnamon sticks and ½ piece of piloncillo (unrefined sugar). Stir to prevent lumps from forming. Remove from heat and stir until the piloncillo has dissolved and the tejuino reaches the desired texture.

TONIC 77

PASCAL
ORIZABA 203 COL. ROMA NORTE,
ALCALDÍA CUAUHTÉMOC

This Gin & Tonic uses a Mexican gin made from green prickly pear cactus. From the first sip you'll find an explosion of freshness and acidity with the twist of a beautiful pink color of the pink prickly pear, also known as tuna rosa.

GLASSWARE: Balloon gin glass
GARNISH: Dehydrated lemon wheel

- 2 oz. | 60 ml Gin Fresco 77
- 1 oz. | 30 ml Pink Prickly Pear Shrub (see recipe)
- ½ oz. | 15 ml fresh lime juice
- ½ oz. | 15 ml citrus cordial
- 2 oz. | 60 ml tonic water, to top

1. Combine all of the ingredients, except for the tonic water, in a cocktail shaker filled with ice.

2. Shake vigorously until chilled and strain the cocktail into a balloon gin glass filled with ice.

3. Top with tonic water and garnish with a dehydrated lemon wheel.

PINK PRICKLY PEAR SHRUB: Add 250 grams (1⅔ cups) pink prickly pear, 3 grams (1 teaspoon) pink pepper, and 50 ml (1¾ oz.) water to a blender and blend until mixed. Strain the mixture to remove seeds and residue, then add 125 ml (4 oz.) apple cider vinegar and 225 grams (1 cup) sugar and stir until the sugar dissolves. Store it in a container, add 2 pieces of lemon peel, and let it rest for 2 days.

GALLITO

In Mexico, we say *¡Ponte Gallo!* to start our day with confidence and a bold spirit. Crafted in Rayo, number 17 on North America's 50 Best Bars 2023, this cocktail is a Garibaldi variation that pays tribute to the stands along CDMX streets selling fresh fruit juices in the morning. So, get ready to enjoy a Gallito and embrace life fearlessly.

GLASSWARE: Wineglass

GARNISH: Orange wedge or rooster chip

- 2 oz. | 60 ml orange juice
- 2 oz. | 60 ml pineapple juice
- 1 oz. | 30 ml mezcal
- 1 oz. | 30 ml Campari
- ½ oz. | 15 ml rum
- ½ oz. | 15 ml fresh lime juice
- ½ oz. | 15 ml strawberry-raspberry syrup

1. Combine all of the ingredients in a cocktail shaker.
2. Dry-shake vigorously.
3. Strain the cocktail into a wineglass filled with ice cubes.
4. Garnish with an orange wedge or rooster chip.

MARTINI DE HOJA SANTA

SALÓN ROSETTA
COLIMA 166, COL. ROMA NORTE,
ALCALDÍA CUAUHTÉMOC

William Hetzel has been a head bartender in the finest bars globally, and at Salón Rosetta he found a cozy place in the heart of Mexico City where the cocktails are made with the best Mexican ingredients. This dry Martini maintains its original essence and gets a boost from the anise, eucalyptus, and mint notes that come from the incorporation of the hoja santa fragrance.

GLASSWARE: Martini glass

GARNISH: Candied hoja santa

- 1¾ oz. | 52.5 ml gin

- ½ oz. | 15 ml Dry Vermouth Infused with Hoja Santa (see recipe)

1. Combine all of the ingredients in a mixing glass with ice.

2. Stir until chilled.

3. Strain the cocktail into the martini glass.

4. Garnish with a candied hoja santa.

DRY VERMOUTH INFUSED WITH HOJA SANTA: Add 10 grams hoja santa to 1 (750 ml) bottle dry vermouth. Let it infuse in the refrigerator for 24 hours. Strain and set aside.

TLECAN

ALVARO OBREGÓN 228 LOCAL 2, COL. ROMA NORTE, ALCALDÍA CUAUHTÉMOC

Tlecan, which means "Place of Fire" in Náhuatl, is a place that show-cases the diversity of mezcal while honoring centuries of tradition and history. Its mystical and enchanting atmosphere transports visitors back to the pre-Hispanic era, with a reddish-brown structure, flickering candles, and the smoke of copal. A replica of the Aztec Disco de la Muerte, or Disk of Mictlantecutli, stands as an homage to Tenochtitlán and its culture. "Tlecan is an experience that engages all the senses: sight, touch, smell," says co-owner Eli Martínez Bello. "We have copal incense burning, providing a sacred aroma, and the lighting is set in a certain way to create a complete sensory experience."

Eli brought her expertise in fine dining from her previous experi-ence at world-renowned Pujol to elevate Tlecan's overall hospitality. The bartenders have participated in training sessions to elevate Tle-can's guests' experience, such as learning the ancient Náhuatl lan-guage, voice placement classes with a broadcaster, and corporal expression classes with a ballet dancer. "It goes beyond serving drinks and good mezcals; it's about having people who are completely proud to be Mexican, to learn new things, to see them grow."

At Tlecan, guests not only enjoy delightful mezcal from various Mexican states or signature cocktails, but they also immerse them-selves in an experience of Mexican hospitality where cultural apprecia-tion shines with passion and pride to create a truly special bar.

PALOMA BLANCA

TLECAN
ALVARO OBREGÓN 228 LOCAL 2, COL. ROMA NORTE,
ALCALDÍA CUAUHTÉMOC

Tlecan is an enigmatic bar where the copal incense blends with the traditional Mexican spirits, cocktails, and culture. The Paloma Blanca emerges as a minimalistic and sophisticated reinterpretation of the classic Paloma, using mezcal for a twist.

GLASSWARE: Highball glass

GARNISH: Grapefruit half-moon

- Starfruit Salt (see recipe), for the rim
- 3 oz. | 90 ml Clarified & Carbonated Grapefruit Juice (see recipe)
- ¾ oz. | 22.5 ml Clarified Lime Juice (see recipe)
- 1⅓ oz. | 40 ml Mezcal Espadín Capón 2 Years
- ½ oz. | 15 ml sparkling water

1. Wet the rim of a highball glass and dip it into the Starfruit Salt.
2. Build the cocktail, in the order listed, in the highball over one large rectangular ice cube.
3. Stir gently to combine.
4. Garnish with a half-moon of grapefruit.

STARFRUIT SALT: Add sea salt and starfruit juice in a container and mix thoroughly. Spread the mixture on wax paper and let it dehydrate.

CLARIFIED & CARBONATED GRAPEFRUIT JUICE: Heat 100 ml (3⅓ oz.) grapefruit juice with 2 grams (1 teaspoon) agar agar, stirring until the agar agar is dissolved. Add 100 grams (3½ oz.) sugar and 5 grams (1 teaspoon) citric acid with 900 ml (3¾ cups) grapefruit juice. Combine this with the agar agar grapefruit juice mixture. Freeze for 10 minutes and strain it. Season it with 5 grams (¾ teaspoon) salt and 1 gram (¼ teaspoon) citric acid. Carbonate it with a Sodastream or other carbonating machine.

CLARIFIED LIME JUICE: Heat 100 ml (3⅓ oz.) water with 2 grams (1 teaspoon) agar agar, and stir until dissolved. Add 400 ml (1⅔ cups) lime juice to the agar agar water. Freeze for 10 minutes. Strain it.

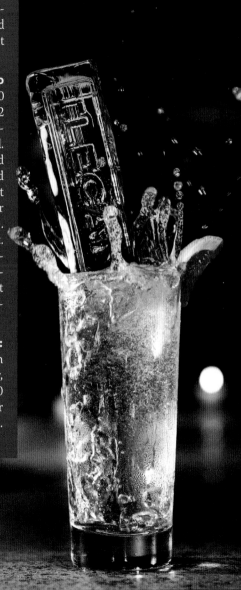

WILSON MAI TAI

CASA PRUNES
CHIHUAHUA 78, COL. ROMA NORTE,
ALCALDÍA CUAUHTÉMOC

Set in an impressive Art Nouveau mansion, Casa Prunes offers several experiences including a cigar lounge, chef's table, speakeasy, laboratories, mixology, or cooking workshops, as well as an agave lounge. Inspired by the Tom Hanks movie *Cast Away*, this reinterpretation of the Mai Tai is the only thing you'll need if you find yourself stranded on an island!

GLASSWARE: Collins glass

GARNISH: Chocolate Wilson (see recipe), Butter Cookie Island (see recipe), banana leaf

---

- 1½ oz. | 45 ml Orgeat Peanut with Sesame Seed (see recipe)
- ½ oz. | 15 ml Rum Zacapa Ámbar
- ½ oz. | 15 ml Appleton Estate Signature Jamaica Rum
- ½ oz. | 15 ml Bacardí Reserva Ocho
- ½ oz. | 15 ml Alma Finca Orange Liqueur
- ½ oz. | 15 ml fresh lemon juice
- ½ oz. | 15 ml fresh lime juice

1. Combine all of the ingredients in a cocktail shaker filled with ice.
2. Shake vigorously until chilled and strain the cocktail into a collins glass filled with crushed ice.
3. Garnish with Chocolate Wilson over a Butter Cookie Island and banana leaf.

ORGEAT PEANUT WITH SESAME SEED: Toast 1 kilogram (2⅕ pounds) salted peanuts at 352°F (160°C) for 25 minutes. Once cooled, grind the peanuts with 450 ml (2 cups) sesame oil. Set aside. Add 2 liters (8 cups) water and 54 grams (⅓ cup) oriental spice tea into a saucepan and infuse the tea, then strain it. Add 1.8 kilograms (4 pounds) sugar and 200 ml (6¾ oz.) almond milk to the tea. Combine one-third of this infused mixture with the peanut and sesame mixture. Freeze for 5 hours to integrate the ingredients.

BUTTER COOKIE ISLAND: Combine 220 grams (2 sticks) butter at room temperature, 2 grams (¼ teaspoon) salt, 290 grams (1½ cups) sugar, 400 grams (2½ cups) flour, and 2 eggs. Once the dough is ready, divide it into four portions and shape them into rolls. Refrigerate for 5 hours. Shape the dough as desired and bake at 266°F (130°C) for 18 minutes.

CHOCOLATE WILSON: Create a mixture with 6 egg yolks and 100 grams (¾ cup) maizena (cornstarch). Simultaneously, heat 500 ml (2 cups) coconut milk and 500 ml (2 cups) coconut cream in a saucepan. Combine both parts. Place the mixture in a mold with the shape desired and freeze it for 5 hours. Once ready, coat the mixture in white chocolate liquid. Let it chill for 5 minutes in the refrigerator, and then, using edible paint, draw the shape of Wilson.

GIMLET

CASA PRUNES
CHIHUAHUA 78, COL. ROMA NORTE, ALCALDÍA CUAUHTÉMOC

Casa Prunes is at the top of the list of places where professional bartenders and cocktail enthusiasts love to visit for a drink, where classic cocktails are reinterpreted using house-made ingredients.

GLASSWARE: Nick & Nora glass

GARNISH: Guava Granita (see recipe)

- 1½ oz. | 45 ml Lime-Infused Gin (see recipe)
- ½ oz. | 15 ml Acid Mix (see recipe)
- ½ oz. | 15 ml Lemongrass Syrup (see recipe)

1. Chill a Nick & Nora glass. Combine all of the ingredients in a cocktail shaker filled with ice.
2. Shake vigorously until chilled.
3. Double-strain the cocktail into the chilled Nick & Nora.
4. Garnish with a scoop of guava granita.

LIME-INFUSED GIN: Add 10 kaffir lime leaves to 1 (750 ml) bottle of Gin Las Californias Cítrico. Let the bottle infuse, in cold water, for 14 hours. Strain and reserve the gin.

ACID MIX: Add 10 grams (2 teaspoons) citric acid, 4 grams (1 teaspoon) malic acid, 3 grams (½ teaspoon) tartaric acid, 2 grams (½ teaspoon) ascorbic acid into 1 liter (4 cups) water. Dissolve the powders and set aside.

LEMONGRASS SYRUP: Place 250 grams dried lemongrass into 750 ml (3 cups) simple syrup in a saucepan over medium heat. Let it infuse and remove from heat just before the syrup boils. Place the mixture in a cold water bath for thermal shock. Strain and reserve the syrup.

GUAVA GRANITA: Add 13 grams ice-cream stabilizer, 30 grams powdered milk, 50 grams dextrose, and 500 ml (2 cups) guava juice to a pot. Bring the mixture to a boil. Place the mixture in a cold water bath for thermal shock. Transfer to an ice cream maker and churn for 40 minutes.

OROPEL'S VERMOUTH REVOLUTION IN CDMX

CHIHUAHUA 182 COL. ROMA NORTE, ALCALDÍA CUAUHTÉMOC

Vermouth, often spelled "vermut" in Spanish, is a fortified wine to which botanicals—herbs and spices—are added to create a bittersweet flavor profile. Commonly consumed as an aperitif, vermouth is a very common ingredient in cocktails.

Oropel's walls, painted in a vibrant shade of yellow, serve as a nod to its name, a decorative foil that resembles a gold leaf often used to decorate ancient objects. As the first vermouth bar in Mexico City, Oropel (@oropelcdmx) stands as a pioneer in the local scene, offering not just vermouths but also cocktails, without losing its focus as a ver-mutería. Irina Maximowitsch, one of the four founders, explains that Oropel's approach "goes beyond what the vermouth adds to the cock-tail; it's about integrating vermouth into everything we have in the bar."

Irina continues: "Over the years, Mexico has seen the rise and fall of several drinking trends boosted by different brands. In the early 2000s there was an increase in popularity of whiskeys and bourbons, such as JB, Johnnie Walker, or Jack Daniel's, followed by Absolut's vodka reign. More recently we have experienced a significant expansion in the con-sumption of mezcal, tequila, gin, and Spritz cocktails. Today, the trend is shifting toward different wine categories, including natural wine that with its unique labels and minimal intervention practices has been growing [an] appreciation for more artisanal beverages. As Mexico's palate continues to evolve, it's evident that lower alcohol-by-volume (ABV) products, and new flavors such as vermouth, will contribute to generate culture and appreciation for refined drinking experiences," Irina says.

Make sure to raise your glass with Irina, Fernanda, Ramses, and Bogar, Oropel's founders, and join its vermouth revolution in Mexico City.

OROPEL

OROPEL
CHIHUAHUA 182 COL. ROMA NORTE,
ALCALDÍA CUAUHTÉMOC

This cocktail is a delicately balanced, non-sweet variation of a Martini, without the intensity found in traditional gin- or vodka-based Martinis.

GLASSWARE: Vintage coupe glass
GARNISH: Lemon zest

- 1½ oz. | 45 ml dry vermouth
- 1½ oz. | 45 ml white vermouth
- 3 dashes orange bitters

1. Chill a vintage coupe glass. Combine all of the ingredients in a mixing glass filled with 5 to 6 ice cubes.
2. Stir for 20 seconds until chilled.
3. Strain the cocktail into the chilled coupe.
4. Garnish with lemon zest.

OZAIN

In the Yoruba religion, Ozain is a deity, the guardian of the secrets of herbs and plants used in traditional African medicine. Fabián Muñoz created this cocktail, in which the combination of botanicals in the absinthe adds highly aromatic notes, as a tribute to Ozain.

GLASSWARE: Rocks glass

GARNISH: Lime twist, fresh rosemary

- 5 grams fresh ginger
- ½ oz. | 15 ml fresh lime juice
- 1½ oz. | 45 ml La Gloria Ron Añejo Tequila
- ½ oz. | 15 ml Cinzano Rosso
- ½ oz. | 15 ml simple syrup
- 10 drops Green Tree Absinth Fairy
- Lime peel, to aromatize

1. Chill a rocks glass. Cut the ginger into pieces and place them in a cocktail shaker with lime juice and muddle.
2. Add the remaining ingredients, except for the lime peel, and shake vigorously with ice.
3. Double-strain the cocktail into the chilled rocks glass filled with ice cubes.
4. Aromatize with the lime peel and discard the peel. Garnish with a lime twist and fresh rosemary.

TÉ DE CHARLIE

SARTORIA
ORIZABA 42, COL. ROMA NORTE,
ALCALDÍA CUAUHTÉMOC

Charlie has been the bartender at Sartoria since just after it opened its doors. He crafted the enigmatic "Charlie's Tea" inspired by the warm spring afternoons of March and April in Mexico City. Currently, this classic remains a well-known secret, since it doesn't appear on the menu; however, those who know about this hidden gem can still enjoy it upon request.

GLASSWARE: Wineglass
GARNISH: Orange twist

- 2 oz. | 60 ml gin
- 1 oz. | 30 ml St-Germain Elderflower Liqueur
- 1 oz. | 30 ml orange juice
- ½ oz. | 15 ml fresh lime juice
- 1 oz. | 30 ml sparkling wine, to top

1. Combine all of the ingredients, except for the sparkling wine, in a cocktail shaker filled with ice.
2. Shake vigorously until chilled and strain over ice cubes into a wineglass.
3. Top with sparkling wine and garnish with an orange twist.

MILLE

POLPO
ÁLVARO OBREGÓN 130 (PASAJE PARIÁN) COL.
ROMA NORTE, ALCALDÍA CUAUHTÉMOC

Polpo has been characterized by having a menu where you can always find something new, from food to cocktails. Mille is a well-balanced drink, with aromas of flower and citrus notes, without leaving behind the velvety texture of a Sour.

GLASSWARE: Coupette glass
GARNISH: Fresh chamomile flowers

- 2 oz. | 60 ml chamomile tea, cooled
- 1 oz. | 30 ml mezcal
- 1 oz. | 30 ml orange juice
- 1 oz. | 30 ml egg white

1. Combine all of the ingredients in a cocktail shaker and dry-shake to foam the egg white, then add ice and shake again.
2. Strain the cocktail into a coupette.
3. Garnish with fresh chamomile flowers.

LAWER

THE MIDNIGHT MONKEY
PLAZA RÍO DE JANEIRO 54, COL. ROMA NORTE, ALCALDÍA CUAUHTÉMOC

The Midnight Monkey brings the hedonism of the 1920s and the golden era of jazz and blues to the heart of Roma Norte. Their specialty cocktails recall the Prohibition Era and the spirits used stay true to that time. Designed by Diego Falcón, Lawer is a cocktail where each ingredient serves a purpose and carries meaning. The fig leaf, for example, represents the evolution of humanity on earth, allowing it to constantly evolve.

GLASSWARE: Highball glass

GARNISH: Fig leaf, Amarena cherry

- 2 oz. | 60 ml Butter Fat–Washed Cognac (see recipe)
- 1 oz. | 30 ml Amarena Syrup (see recipe)
- 1 oz. | 30 ml Fig Leaf Redistillation (see recipe)
- 1½ oz. | 45 ml pennyroyal soda, to top

1. Combine all of the ingredients, except for the soda, in a cocktail shaker filled with ice.
2. Shake vigorously until chilled.
3. Double-strain the cocktail into a highball filled with ice and top with the soda.
4. Garnish with a fig leaf and an Amarena cherry.

BUTTER FAT–WASHED COGNAC: Melt 450 ml unsalted butter in a saucepan and let it cool. Combine the mixture with 1 (750 ml) bottle of Martell Blue Swift. Allow the mixture to freeze until the butter solidifies. Strain the cognac through a fine-mesh strainer.

AMARENA SYRUP: Place Amarena cherry juice and equal parts sugar and water in a saucepan. Bring the mixture to a boil, lower the heat, and reduce until syrupy. Strain and reserve the syrup.

FIG LEAF REDISTILLATION: Combine 300 grams (10 oz.) fig leaves with 1 liter (4 cups) white wine. Heat the mixture, allowing it to infuse. Let it cool, then strain and bottle the wine.

2244

SOMBRA
ORIZABA 96, COL. ROMA NORTE,
ALCALDÍA CUAUHTÉMOC

Sombra ("shadow") is a planet where rebels and dreamers live in a corner of a distant galaxy in the year 2244 AAI (After Artificial Intelligence). Hence the cocktail's name. It's a relaxed yet futuristic speakeasy where enigma and mystique blend with sophisticated, sustainable, and minimalist cocktails. Created by Adrian López, this cocktail is based on the concept of a crystal that controls time and space that will allow you to travel from earth to the Shadow Planet in the year 2244.

GLASSWARE: Rocks glass

GARNISH: Ardbeg Wee Bestie spritz

- 2 oz. | 60 ml Filtered Apple Juice (see recipe)
- 1¾ oz. | 52.5 ml Ginstone
- ½ oz. | 15 ml simple syrup
- ½ oz. | 15 ml Citric Acid Solution (see recipe)
- ⅙ oz. | 5 ml Giffard Menthe-Pastille

1. Combine all of the ingredients in a mixing glass filled with ice.

2. Stir until chilled, then strain the cocktail over ice into a rocks glass.

3. Spritz the top of the drink with scotch.

FILTERED APPLE JUICE: Filter apple juice, as needed, through a cheesecloth or napkin fast to prevent oxidation and achieve a translucent liquid.

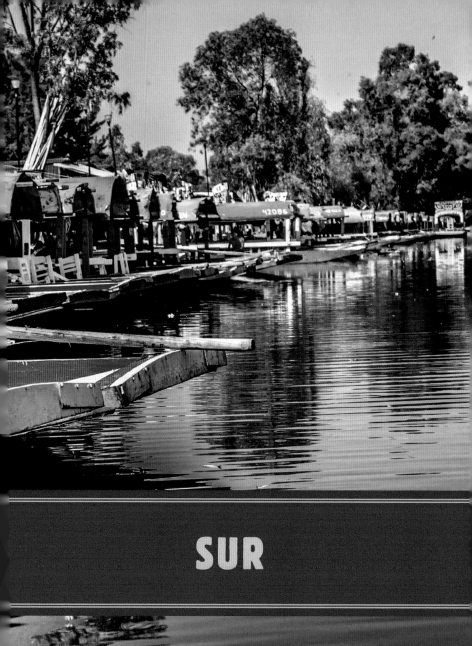

SUR

EL CAIRO

LAVENDER

MARÍA BONITA

SUPERNOVA

GODZILLA

PITUFO 2.0

CARAJILLO CRIOLLO

MEZCAL PUNCH

MEZCALITA XIPE

From the historic and colonial neighborhoods of Coyoacán and San Ángel to the canals of Xochimilco, the southern part of Mexico City has its own enchanting beauty. It was here that Frida Kahlo and Diego Rivera found inspiration in the colorful streets, and where markets, artwork, squares, and fountains will immerse you in a cultural hub.

Get ready to discover a Mexican cocktail scene true to its roots, where traditional flavors are integrated with the art of mixology, resulting in unique drinks. And just remember the popular saying: *Para todo mal, mezcal, y para todo bien también*, which means, "For everything bad, mezcal, and for everything good, the same."

¡Salud!/Cheers!

EL CAIRO

ALAIA TERRAZA
CDA. CANOA 80 COLONIA TIZAPÁN SAN ÁNGEL,
ALCALDÍA ÁLVARO OBREGÓN

Luis Franklin Hernández is the genius behind this creation. Inspired by a harmonious fusion of aromas and flavors, intricate techniques and textures, and the exquisite blend of exotic spices and ingredients, it effortlessly transports you, with a sip, to distant lands. Orange mead (*hidromiel* in Spanish) is a beverage crafted from honey and water, fermented with yeast and infused with orange peels.

GLASSWARE: Rocks glass

GARNISH: Lavender flowers, basil flowers

- 1½ oz. | 45 ml tequila reposado
- 1 oz. | 30 ml Clarified Pineapple Juice (see recipe)
- 1 oz. | 30 ml Orange Mead (see recipe)
- 1 oz. | 30 ml chamomile tea, cooled
- ½ oz. | 15 ml Anubis Mixer (see recipe)

1. Combine all of the ingredients in a cocktail shaker filled with ice.

2. Mix the ingredients using the throwing technique.

3. Strain the cocktail into a rocks glass over an ice sphere.

4. Garnish with lavender and basil flowers.

ORANGE MEAD: In a large jar, combine 500 ml (2 cups) honey, 1.5 liters (6 cups) water, and 2 grams yeast. Allow the mixture to ferment. Add the peels of 2 navel oranges for flavor.

CLARIFIED PINEAPPLE JUICE: Blend fresh pineapple chunks, as needed, until smooth. Strain the blended pineapple through a fine-mesh sieve or cheesecloth to remove any pulp, leaving you with clear pineapple juice. Alternatively, you can use a centrifuge or gelatin-fining process for further clarification if you desire an exceptionally clear juice.

ANUBIS MIXER: Reduce Liquore Strega to intensify its flavor in a saucepan over low heat. Then, infuse it with the zest of Eureka lemons, lemongrass, lavender, and rosemary. Allow the mixture to steep before straining, resulting in a fragrant and flavorful mixer perfect for enhancing cocktails with a unique herbal and citrus twist.

LAVENDER

BARRA 975
PL. SAN JACINTO 11, COLONIA SAN ÁNGEL,
ALCALDÍA ÁLVARO OBREGÓN

Michelle Ogando and Antonio Poveda embarked on a remarkable journey to create contemporary mixology that bridges the classic and the artisanal. Their inspiration revolves around three essentials: color, flavor, and a profound understanding of the ingredients' origins, as you'll discover in this cocktail.

GLASSWARE: Rocks glass
GARNISH: Fresh lavender flowers

- Lavender Salt (see recipe), for the rim
- 1½ oz. | 45 ml tequila
- 1 oz. | 30 ml Love & Blackberries Infusion (see recipe)
- ½ oz. | 15 ml blue curaçao
- ½ oz. | 15 ml fresh lemon juice
- ½ oz. | 15 ml simple syrup

1. Wet the rim of the rocks glass and dip it into the Lavender Salt. Set aside.
2. Combine all of the ingredients in a cocktail shaker filled with ice.
3. Shake vigorously until chilled and strain the cocktail over ice cubes into the salt-rimmed rocks glass.
4. Garnish with lavender flowers.

LAVENDER SALT: Add a mixture of 90 percent coarse sea salt and 10 percent dehydrated lavender seeds to a mortar and pestle. Grind the ingredients together.

LOVE & BLACKBERRIES INFUSION: Infuse 5 grams (½ oz.) hibiscus, 5 grams (1 tablespoon) cloves, and 5 grams (or 2) blackberries in 250 ml (1 cup) hot water for 5 minutes. Strain it and reserve it.

MARÍA BONITA

CORAZÓN DE MAGUEY
JARDÍN CENTENARIO 9-A, COL. VILLA COYOACÁN,
ALCALDÍA COYOACÁN

A temple devoted to Mayahuel, the goddess of maguey, where the costumes of Tehuacán dancers, *damajuanas*, and intricate engravings transport you on a journey to savor the rich Mexican heritage. Crafted by renowned mixologist Claudia Cabrera Rodríguez, this cocktail unveils the delightful aromas and flavors of Mexican spirits, accompanied by a truly unique garnish: grasshoppers and guacamole.

GLASSWARE: Highball glass

GARNISH: Chalupa with grasshoppers and guacamole

- Hibiscus Salt (see recipe), for the rim
- 3 oz. | 90 ml Clamato
- 1½ oz. | 45 ml Avocado Leaf–Infused Mezcal (see recipe)
- 1 oz. | 30 ml red salsa
- ½ oz. | 15 ml Fernet-Branca
- ½ oz. | 15 ml sauces mix
- Few drops avocado bitters

1. Wet the rim of a highball glass and dip it into the Hibiscus Salt.
2. Combine all of the ingredients in a cocktail shaker filled with ice.
3. Shake vigorously until chilled then strain the cocktail over ice into the highball.
4. Garnish with a chalupa with grasshoppers and guacamole.

HIBISCUS SALT: Combine 50 grams (2 oz.) salt with 50 grams (2 oz.) dried hibiscus in a grinder and process until finely ground.

AVOCADO LEAF–INFUSED MEZCAL: Place 1 (750 ml) bottle Alipús San Baltazar Mezcal and 40 grams (1½ oz.) avocado leaf in a vacuum bag. Use a vacuum machine to seal the bag and ensure there are no leaks. Set the sous vide to 147.2°F (64°C), and once it reaches temperature, put the bag in and leave it for 30 minutes. Remove from the sous vide, open the bag, strain, and refrigerate it.

SUPERNOVA

Javier Alvarado captured the essence of both Mexican and French cultures in this cocktail, achieving a unique balance and contrast of flavors between mezcal and Champagne. Here the blue color not only adds a visual touch, it also represents the distinctive Novotel color, where Bar Delia is located.

GLASSWARE: Highball glass

GARNISH: Lime peel, lemongrass

- 1 oz. | 30 ml Mezcal Trascendente Espadín
- ¾ oz. | 22.5 ml St-Germain Elderflower Liqueur
- ¾ oz. | 22.5 ml Gin Armónico
- ¼ oz. | 7.5 ml Malic Citrus Cordial (see recipe)
- Blueberry Tincture (see recipe), as needed
- Champagne, to top

1. Combine all of the ingredients, except for the Champagne and Blueberry Tincture, in a mixing glass filled with ice.
2. Stir until chilled and strain the cocktail into a highball filled with ice cubes.
3. Top with Champagne and slowly add the tincture with a barspoon, creating a layer ½ in. (2 cm) thick on top of the highball.
4. Garnish with a lime peel and lemongrass.

MALIC CITRUS CORDIAL:

Add 500 ml (2 cups) simple syrup, 30 grams (2 tablespoons) citric acid powder, and 30 grams (2 tablespoons) malic acid powder to a bowl. Mix until a homogeneous mixture is achieved. Bottle it and let it rest for 24 hours. Note: All of this preparation is done cold or at room temperature.

BLUEBERRY TINCTURE:

Add lemongrass, chamomile, natural lavender leaf, blue algae, cardamom, pink pepper, and macerated blueberry in a container filled with water. Let it infuse at room temperature for 24 hours. Bring it to a boil to extract all possible tinctures. Once the mixture reaches room temperature, strain and reserve it.

GODZILLA

KAITO DEL VALLE
PESTALOZZI 1238, COL. DEL VALLE,
ALCALDÍA BENITO JUÁREZ

R anked at number 23 among North America's 50 Best Bars in 2023, this is the first Latin American all-woman bar team, led by the magnificent Claudia Cabrera Rodríguez. Inspired by a fusion of Japanese izakayas and Mexican influences, their cocktails are full of creativity, starting with the ingredients and the visual elements. At first, Godzilla was quite complicated to sell at Kaito, as not all Mexicans love wasabi; nevertheless, once they tried it, they noticed how fresh, easy to drink, and citrusy this cocktail is, swiftly transforming it into one of the spot's favorites.

*

GLASSWARE: Godzilla mug

GARNISH: Dehydrated peas with wasabi in a cone, Citric Dust
(see recipe)

- 2 oz. | 60 ml sake
- 2 oz. | 60 ml Lemongrass Solution (see recipe)
- 1 oz. | 30 ml Wasabi Syrup (see recipe)
- 1 oz. | 30 ml gin
- ½ oz. | 15 ml fresh lime juice

1. Combine all of the ingredients in a cocktail shaker filled with ice.

2. Shake vigorously until chilled.

3. Strain the cocktail over ice into a Godzilla mug.

4. Garnish with dehydrated peas with wasabi in a cone and Citric Dust.

LEMONGRASS SOLUTION: In a pot add 150 grams (5 oz.) lemongrass and 500 ml (2 cups) water and bring the mixture to a boil. Remove the pot from heat and let the mixture cool. Once it's cool, strain the solution.

WASABI SYRUP: In a pot, add 500 grams (1 pound) sugar and 500 ml (2 cups) water. Bring the mixture to a boil, allowing it to reduce until you achieve a syrup-like consistency, and then add wasabi, to taste. Combine the mixture, let it cool, and reserve it.

CITRIC DUST: Using citrus peels from previously used oranges, grapefruits, limes, and lemons, dehydrate and process the mixture until it is transformed into dust.

RUMORES BUTCHER SHOP

INSURGENTES SUR 1839, COL. GUADALUPE INN, ALCALDÍA ÁLVARO OBREGÓN

Mexico City has a special love for speakeasies, inspired by the clandestine bars of the Prohibition Era. In early 2012, the first Mexico City speakeasy opened its doors right in the heart of Polanquito. Jule's Basement, whose entrance was through an industrial refrigerator inside Surtidora's Don Bátiz restaurant, was a small place with exceptional mixology. Soon after, other speakeasies arrived on the scene, such as Xaman, Hanky Panky, Parker & Lenox, and Handshake, the last of which opened in 2023 and placed third in The World's 50 Best Bars. Nowadays, the concept has been exported not only to secret bars, but also to mysterious restaurants and bakeries too. Because CDMX!

One of the most recent openings is Rumores Butcher Shop, a speakeasy nestled in Sur. Don't be fooled by the facade of a butcher shop. Behind this store, a world of signature cocktails awaits, but make sure you know the secret password . . .

Here, the past and tradition meets with the future and innovation—once you enter, you'll find two different bars. One (future) features cocktails that use special techniques with rotavaps and gasifiers. At the back, a second bar (past) offers interesting interpretations of classic cocktails.

PITUFO 2.0

RUMORES BUTCHER SHOP
INSURGENTES SUR 1839, COL. GUADALUPE INN,
ALCALDÍA ÁLVARO OBREGÓN

This drink is inspired by a typical preparation for the popular Azulito, better known as Destilado de los Pitufos, or Smurf Distillate, due to its blue color.

GLASSWARE: Highball glass
GARNISH: False Cherry (see recipe)

- 1½ oz. | 45 ml citrus-flavored vodka
- ¾ oz. | 22.5 ml Pitufo's Cordial (see recipe)
- ½ oz. | 15 ml citric solution
- ½ oz. | 15 ml lemon oleo saccharum
- 2 oz. | 60 ml Lime Soda (see recipe)

1. Build the cocktail in the order of ingredients listed in a highball filled with ice cubes.
2. Stir until chilled and garnish with the False Cherry.

PITUFO'S CORDIAL: Combine lemon oil, grape flavoring, tartaric acid, citric acid, and blue edible food coloring in a 2:1 ratio with simple syrup. Reserve two parts: one for the main cocktail and the second for the False Cherry (see recipe).

LIME SODA: Let lime, lemon, and orange peels, as needed, steep in water for 2 days. Strain the mixture and carbonate it with a soda maker.

FALSE CHERRY: Take the Pitufo's Cordial (see recipe), lime oil, malic acid, and cherry flavoring and reduce it in a saucepan. Add natural cherry stems. Shape the reduction into the form of a cherry. Dip it into white cocoa colored with edible red food coloring.

CLAUDIA CABRERA RODRÍGUEZ

Claudia Cabrera Rodríguez (@klawklaw) is not only one of the most impressive Mexican mixologists, she is also a great inspiration for future bartenders. An accomplished alchemist, Claudia's passion for mixology began in her twenties. While working in restaurants, she developed an interest in wine and classic cocktails that led her to Canada. It was in Vancouver, where she trained at the Metropolitan Bartending School, that she deepened her knowledge of spirits, liquors, and the art of crafting cocktails. When she returned to Mexico, her passion for Mexican ancestral spirits such as mezcal was awakened, as was her competitive side, and she went on to win six national titles.

She became involved with Kaito, helping the all-woman bar team rank 26 in North America's 50 Best Bars 2023. She served as a brand ambassador for Fernet-Branca and is currently an advisor to several gastronomic projects in Mexico, such as Los Danzantes, Corazón de Maguey, and SOD, while also serving on the philanthropy and development committee at Tales of the Cocktail.

Claudia has been nominated as Best Bartender and Best Ambassador at Tales of the Cocktail. She has been named Mixologist of the Year by the Mexican gastronomic critic Marco Beteta and by Culinaria Mexicana, and Best Bartender by Casa Cuervo.

With over 600 of her own cocktail creations, Claudia's favorite ingredients to work with include, of course, mezcal, Fernet-Branca, gin, creams, oils, and salts. Her creative process is inspired by her love for food and travel. "I love to eat," she says. "Everything revolves around food for me. I enjoy traveling, and I always carry a little notebook to write down the new flavors I enjoy in each experience. I love to draw, and I have notebooks for each project where I sketch out how my cocktail will look, what ingredients it will contain, as well as ice, garnishes, and more. I brainstorm ingredients, dishes, colors, images, music, just everything, and then I piece together the puzzle."

CARAJILLO CRIOLLO

LOS DANZANTES COYOACÁN
JARDÍN CENTENARIO 12 COL. VILLA COYOACÁN,
ALCALDÍA COYOACÁN

One of the most representative cocktails of Mexico City is, for sure, the Carajillo, a sweet and powerful cocktail served to be paired with desserts or as a digestif. Its original recipe includes Licor 43 and a shot of espresso in equal parts, but Claudia Cabrera Rodríguez's version exceeds the expectations of a classic one. Instead of using Licor 43, a Spanish liqueur characterized by hints of vanilla and spices, Claudia uses Nixta Licor de Elote, a Mexican corn liqueur made from a base of tender cacahuazintle. Certainly, there's nothing that tastes more like home than café de olla, a sweet and spiced coffee that warms everybody's heart, as well as the Mayordomo chocolate, which is a typical Oaxacan delight. And, of course, you'll need mezcal. A pinole cookie is a pre-Hispanic mixture of powdered roasted corn, cacao, anise, and cinnamon. Pinole cookies can be store-bought or homemade.

---

*

GLASSWARE: Rocks glass

GARNISH: Pinole cookie, corn leaf

- 1 oz. | 30 ml Mezcal Los Danzantes Espadín
- 1 oz. | 30 ml Café de Olla Syrup (see recipe)
- 1 oz. | 30 ml espresso

- ½ oz. | 15 ml Nixta Licor de Elote
- 1 oz. | 30 ml Mayordomo Chocolate Cream (see recipe), to top

1. Combine all of the ingredients, except for the chocolate cream, in a cocktail shaker filled with ice.

2. Shake vigorously then strain the cocktail into a rocks glass filled with ice cubes.

3. Top with the chocolate cream and garnish with a pinole cookie and a corn leaf.

CAFÉ DE OLLA SYRUP: Add 1 liter (4 cups) coffee (from a percolator), 500 grams (1 pound) refined sugar, 2 cinnamon sticks, 4 pieces of anise, and 5 pieces of cloves to a saucepan on medium heat and mix to combine. Do not allow the mixture to boil. Add 500 grams (18 ounces, or 3 cones) piloncillo (unrefined sugar cane) and dissolve it until a syrupy consistency is obtained. Let it cool and strain it.

MAYORDOMO CHOCOLATE CREAM: Heat 375 ml (1½ cups) whipping cream and mix it with 150 ml Mayordomo chocolate. Strain through a fine-mesh strainer, then pour it into a cream siphon and add a CO_2 cartridge. Let it rest in the refrigerator for at least 30 minutes.

MEZCAL PUNCH

LOS DANZANTES COYOACÁN
JARDÍN CENTENARIO 12 COL. VILLA COYOACÁN,
ALCALDÍA COYOACÁN

A place built to elevate ancient Mexico and fuse it with the contemporary with every sip, Los Danzantes Coyoacán captures the flavor of a Mexican dance between the past, present, and future. This is where Claudia Cabrera Rodríguez, one of the ten nominees for International Bartender of the Year recognized by the Tales of the Cocktail Foundation in 2020, was inspired to make this mystic mezcal cocktail.

GLASSWARE: Rocks glass
GARNISH: Pineapple gummy, pineapple leaves

• **5 oz. | 150 ml Gasified Mezcal Punch (see recipe)**

1. Pour the Gasified Mezcal Punch into a rocks glass filled with an ice cube of 5 x 5 x 7 cm.

2. Stir until chilled.

3. Garnish with a pineapple gummy and pineapple leaves.

GASIFIED MEZCAL PUNCH: In a large saucepan over medium-low heat, add 1 liter (4 cups) milk, let it reach 176°F (80°C), then remove the pan from heat. Add 300 ml (1¼ cups) lemon juice to the hot milk to curdle the milk, and then add 300 ml (1¼ cups) Lemongrass Syrup (see recipe) and stir to combine. Once the temperature decreases to 104°F (40°C), add 1 (750 ml) bottle of Mezcal Danzantes Joven Espadín and 250 ml (1 cup) Kalani Coconut Liqueur. Transfer the mixture to a closed container and store it for 24 hours at room temperature in a dark place to generate buttermilk. Using a coffee filter or cheesecloth, filter the mixture to obtain a clear liquid. Refrigerate and then add it to a PET bottle and gas with CO_2. Refrigerate it until ready to use.

LEMONGRASS SYRUP: Place 100 grams (3½ oz.) lemongrass and equal parts sugar and water in a saucepan. Bring the mixture to a boil then lower the heat, stirring frequently, and reduce until the mixture becomes syrupy. Strain the syrup before using or storing.

MEZCALITA XIPE

A smoked cocktail that highlights the charred flavor of pineapple, ginger, and cardamom, creating a blend of refreshing notes. At Casa Xipe, the atmosphere and the green hues of the vegetation invite you to have a perfect sunny day with a delicious drink.

GLASSWARE: Rocks glass

GARNISH: Charred pineapple, pineapple spear, ground cardamom

- Worm salt, for the rim
- Totomoxtle powder, for the rim
- 2 oz. | 60 ml Mezcal Espadín Joven Los Danzantes
- 2 oz. | 60 ml Charred Pineapple Juice (see recipe)
- 2 oz. | 60 ml fresh pineapple juice
- ½ oz. | 15 ml Ginger Syrup (see recipe)
- ¼ oz. | 7.5 ml Cointreau
- ¼ oz. | 7.5 ml fresh lime juice

1. Wet the rim of the rocks glass and dip it into the worm salt and the totomoxtle powder.
2. Combine all of the ingredients in a cocktail shaker filled with ice.
3. Shake vigorously until chilled and strain the cocktail into a rocks glass filled with ice.
4. Garnish with charred pineapple, pineapple spear, and ground cardamom.

CHARRED PINEAPPLE JUICE:
Char pineapple cubes, as needed,
then blend them. Reserve the juice.

GINGER SYRUP: Place 100 grams
(3½ oz.) sliced fresh ginger in 500 ml
(2 cups) hot water and add 500
grams (1 pound) sugar. Allow the
ginger to infuse the simple syrup
then strain before using.

MEASUREMENT CONVERSIONS

	1 dash		0.625 ml
	4 dashes		2.5 ml
	1 teaspoon		5 ml
¼ oz.			7.5 ml
⅓ oz.	2 teaspoons		10 ml
½ oz.	3 teaspoons	1 tablespoon	15 ml
⅔ oz.	4 teaspoons		20 ml
¾ oz.			22.5 ml
$^{17}/_{20}$ oz.			25 ml
1 oz.		2 tablespoons	30 ml
1½ oz.		3 tablespoons	45 ml
1¾ oz.			52.5 ml
2 oz.	4 tablespoons	¼ cup	60 ml
8 oz.		1 cup	250 ml
16 oz.	1 pint	2 cups	500 ml
24 oz.		3 cups	750 ml
32 oz.	1 quart	4 cups	1 liter (1,000 ml)

Acknowledgments

If you get to this page, I just want to say: *¡Gracias! ¡Gracias! ¡Gracias!* Thank you for reading and recreating the cocktail recipes of this book. Having the honor of exploring my city through the history of its cocktails and witnessing how much this industry and the Mexican spirits have evolved fills my heart with gratitude and happiness; it's like a perfect dream job come true.

But of course, dreams aren't possible without people who believe in you. So, a big thanks to Lindy Pokorny, Buzz Poole, and Jeremy E. Hauck from Cider Mill Press, without whom this book wouldn't exist. To all the amazing spirit brands, brilliant bartenders, the female power in this industry, public relations reps, chefs, and every host who opened their bar, hotel, cantina, and restaurant for me, thank you!

And last but certainly not least, to my dear family and my parents, Martha and Felipe, thank you for always supporting me. To my partner in crime, Pollo, thank you for joining me on this journey, sipping and visiting the bars together. Michelle, thank you for your unconditional support. And to my lovely friends, thank you for always been so cheerful and pushing me to take a next step! Love you all!

As I'm writing these lines while watching a perfect sunset, it feels like a metaphor for finishing this journey. Now that the book is done, every sip, laugh, drink, and meeting with passionate people that love what they do, was all worth it. Each cocktail you'll find here has been a journey in itself and was crafted with the goal of making you live a special moment with a magnificent drink experience.

Tomorrow will be another perfect day to explore new flavors, places and to and try new things. Never lose your curiosity to discover new things. I hope this book inspires you to explore your creative side and continue learning more about cocktails and what Mexico and its spirits have to offer.

With love,
Martha

About the Author

Martha Marquez is a Mexico City–based wine, cocktail, and food writer. Her passion for the beverage industry led her to become a certified sommelier by the Mexican Sommelier Association, with expertise in the field of Chilean wine and spirits. For more than a decade, Martha oversaw the introduction of new Chilean piscos, gins, vodkas, beers, and wines into the Mexican market, and she has also worked to promote Rioja Alavesa and Txakoli wines in Mexico.

Martha's creativity and passion for mixology led her to become the beverage designer for the project Drynk Inc. In 2020, she won first

place in the Sherry Wine Cocktail Contest organized by the INA, showcasing her talent for creating innovative and delicious drinks.

She has also served as ambassador for internationally renowned wine and spirits brands, working on marketing and promotional campaigns. Through her blog @the_ enologist, Martha shares her knowledge of wine, cocktails, travels, events, and food with her audience together with her shiba-inu, Hashi.

Photo Credits

Page 32 courtesy @foodpolicemx, page 37 by Laura Santander, page 43 by Fernando Gómez Carbajal, pages 50, 220, 223 by @zamacona-photo, page 55 by Horacio Rodríguez, page 77 by Andrea David, page 101 by Jack Lindeman, page 113 by Paulina Salazar, page 116 by Viridiana Campos, page 119 by Damián (Taller Astrafilia), page 123 by Alicia Fernández/Gerardo Nava, page 146 by Tomás Marcos, page 149 by Sebastián Anaya, page 162 by Tonatiuh Loredo Bárcenas, page 167 by Araceli Paz (Casamata), page 168 by Eimos D. Ayala Guzmán, page 182 by Laura Santander, page 187 by @_fxalm, page 239 by Rodrigo Bañuelos, pages 244, 246–247, 249 by Wolf Wender and Juan Pablo Cèlis, pages 33, 254, 257 by Bogar Adame Mendoza, page 258 by Raúl González Castillo, pages 261, 262 by Alejandra Nava Moya, page 273 Michelle Ogando, pages 275, 279, 284, 287, 289 by Carlos Castillo, and page 291 by Damián Chiappe.

Pages 9, 14, courtesy of Library of Congress.

Pages 1, 3, 4–5, 6–7, 11, 16–17, 18, 19, 23, 30–31, 34, 38–39, 60–61, 80–81, 96–97, 126–127, 198–199, 266–267 used under official license from Shutterstock.com.

All other images courtesy of the respective bars, restaurants, and interviewees.

Cabuya (in La Condesa)

Index

–ABOUT CIDER MILL PRESS BOOK PUBLISHERS–

Good ideas ripen with time. From seed to harvest, Cider Mill Press brings fine reading, information, and entertainment together between the covers of its creatively crafted books. Our Cider Mill bears fruit twice a year, publishing a new crop of titles each spring and fall.

"Where Good Books Are Ready for Press"
501 Nelson Place
Nashville, Tennessee 37214
cidermillpress.com

Sta Cruz

R. de las Nacas

SCA

R. LEO

Rio de las

Sauced

R. Sauceda

Guadiana

Otomies

Durango

Palos

L. Salso

PANU

S. Martin S.

Munille

Piasda

Chich emecas

Rio Verde

or

S. Ja

Real del Rosario

Sacotecas

Chiametlan

S. Luis de Potosi

Taucaca

e Blas

Teutl

S. Luis de la Paz

GUAS

Sucru

Palioque

mpaque

R. Barania

S. Feline

S. Luis de la Paz

Com.

ostella

Leon

S. Miguel

Queretaro

Mc

Guada laxara

Tula

Tintoque

L. Chapala

Istlan

Salamanca

Salaya

Maylo

Zapodan

MECHO

Mecho acan

MEXICO

Purificacion

Pasquaro

Turiquato

Cuernavaca

Colima

Guanalo

Melin

Tasco

Arenang

Zumyiang

UTH

Naspa

Sihula

Zacatula

Petatlan

ME

Passage

Acapulco